Mastering Text Mining with R

Master text-taming techniques and build effective
text-processing applications with R

Ashish Kumar

Avinash Paul

BIRMINGHAM - MUMBAI

Mastering Text Mining with R

First published: December 2016

Production reference: 1231216

Published by Packt Publishing Ltd.
Livery Place
35 Livery Street
Birmingham B3 2PB, UK.

ISBN 978-1-78355-181-1

www.packtpub.com

Credits

Authors
 Ashish Kumar
 Avinash Paul

Reviewers
 Dmitry Grapov
 Ashraf Uddin

Commissioning Editor
 Kartikey Pandey

Acquisition Editor
 Prachi Bisht

Content DevelopmentEditor
 Mehvash Fatima

Technical Editors
 Akash Patel
 Naveenkumar Jain

Copy Editor
 Safis Editing

Project Coordinator
 Kinjal Bari

Proofreader
 Safis Editing

Indexer
 Rekha Nair

Graphics
 Kirk D'Penha

Production Coordinator
 Shraddha Falebhai

Cover Work
 Shraddha Falebhai

About the Authors

Ashish Kumar is an IIM alumnus and an engineer at heart. He has extensive experience in data science, machine learning, and natural language processing having worked at organizations, such as McAfee-Intel, an ambitious data science startup Volt consulting), and presently associated to the software and research lab of a leading MNC. Apart from work, Ashish also participates in data science competitions at Kaggle in his spare time.

Avinash Paul is a programming language enthusiast, loves exploring open sources technologies and programmer by choice. He has over nine years of programming experience. He has worked in Sabre Holdings , McAfee , Mindtree and has experience in data-driven product development, He was intrigued by data science and data mining while developing niche product in education space for a ambitious data science start-up. He believes data science can solve lot of societal challenges. In his spare time he loves to read technical books and teach underprivileged children back home.

I would like to thank my mother, Anthony Mary, without her continuous support and encouragement I never would have been able to achieve my goals.

About the Reviewers

Dmitry Grapov received his PhD in analytical chemistry with emphasis in biotechnology in 2012 from the University of California, Davis. He currently works as a data scientist at CDS- Creative Data Solutions (`http://createdatasol.com/`) specializing in R programming, machine learning, and data visualization.

Ashraf Uddin has been pursuing PhD at Department of Computer Science, South Asian University (SAU) since July 2013. Before joining PhD, he completed MCA from SAU in June, 2013 (`www.bit.ly/siteAshraf`). He obtained his B.Sc. in Mathematics from the Department of Mathematics, University of Dhaka. He has been working in the area of Scientometrics, Text Data Mining, and Information Extraction.

He has published many journal and conference papers in the area of Scientometrics and Text Analytics. He has also authored a book titled *Applied Information Extraction and Sentiment Analysis.*

I am grateful to my supervisors Dr Pranab Kumar Muhuri and Dr Vivek Kumar Singh for their unconditional support. I also acknowledge my colleagues Rajesh Piryani and Sumit Kumar Banshal for their inspiration and help in the process.

www.PacktPub.com

eBooks, discount offers, and more

Did you know that Packt offers eBook versions of every book published, with PDF and ePub files available? You can upgrade to the eBook version at www.PacktPub.com and as a print book customer, you are entitled to a discount on the eBook copy. Get in touch with us at customercare@packtpub.com for more details.

At www.PacktPub.com, you can also read a collection of free technical articles, sign up for a range of free newsletters and receive exclusive discounts and offers on Packt books and eBooks.

https://www.packtpub.com/mapt

Get the most in-demand software skills with Mapt. Mapt gives you full access to all Packt books and video courses, as well as industry-leading tools to help you plan your personal development and advance your career.

Why subscribe?

- Fully searchable across every book published by Packt
- Copy and paste, print, and bookmark content
- On demand and accessible via a web browser

Customer Feedback

Thank you for purchasing this Packt book. We take our commitment to improving our content and products to meet your needs seriously — that's why your feedback is so valuable. Whatever your feelings about your purchase, please consider leaving a review on this book's Amazon page. Not only will this help us, more importantly it will also help others in the community to make an informed decision about the resources that they invest in to learn.

You can also review for us on a regular basis by joining our reviewers' club. **If you're interested in joining, or would like to learn more about the benefits we offer, please contact us**: customerreviews@packtpub.com.

Table of Contents

Preface

Text Mining is the process of extracting useful and high-quality information from text by devising patterns and trends. R provides an extensive ecosystem to mine text through its many frameworks and packages.

Our aim in this book is to provide you the information that you will use to develop a practical application from the concepts learned and you will understand how text mining can be leveraged to analyze the massively available data on social media.

We hope you'll get as much from reading this book as we did from writing it.

What this book covers

Chapter 1, *Statistical Linguistics with R*, covers the basics of statistical analysis, which forms the basis of computational linguistic. This chapter also discusses about various R packages for text mining and their utilities.

Chapter 2, *Processing Text*, intends to guide readers in handling textual data, right from scratch. Accessing the data from various sources, cleansing texts using Regular expressions, stop words, and help develop skills to process raw texts effectively using R language.

Chapter 3, *Categorizing and Tagging Text*, empowers the readers to categorize the texts into different word classes or lexical categories.

Chapter 4, *Dimensionality Reduction*, covers in detail, the various dimensionality reduction methods that can be applied on text data and extending the concept to extract contexts from data in the next chapter.

Chapter 5, *Text summarization and Clustering*, deals with text summarization and document clustering methods that can be applied to textual documents.

Chapter 6, Text Classification, deals with pattern recognition in text data, using classification mechanism. We will deal with statistical and mathematical aspects along with the implementation on public data sets using R language.

Chapter 7, Entity Recognition, deals with named entity recognition using R and extends the concepts further to the ontology Learning and expansion concepts.

What you need for this book

R 3.3.2 is tested on the following platforms:

- Windows® 7.0 (SP1), 8.1, 10, Windows Server® 2008 R2 (SP1) and 2012
- Ubuntu 14.04, 16.04
- CentOS / Red Hat Enterprise Linux 6.5, 7.1
- SUSE Linux Enterprise Server 11
- Mavericks (10.9), Yosemite (10.10), El Capitan (10.11), Sierra (10.12)

The hardware specification required for this book is as follows:

- Processor: Processor 64-bit processor with x86-compatible architecture (such as AMD64, Intel 64, x86-64, IA-32e, EM64T, or x64 chips). ARM chips, Itanium-architecture chips (also known as IA-64), and non-Intel Macs are not supported. Multiple-core chips are recommended.
- Free disk space. 250 MB.
- RAM. 1 GB required, 4 GB recommended.

Who this book is for

If you are an R programmer, analyst, or data scientist who wants to gain experience in performing text data mining and analytic with R, then this book is for you. Experience of working with statistical methods and language processing would be helpful.

Conventions

In this book, you will find a number of text styles that distinguish between different kinds of information. Here are some examples of these styles and an explanation of their meaning.

Code words in text, database table names, folder names, filenames, file extensions, path names, dummy URLs, user input, and Twitter handles are shown as follows: "We can include other contexts through the use of the `include` directive."

A block of code is set as follows:

```
library(prob)
S <- rolldie(2, makespace = TRUE)
A <- subset(S, X1 + X2 >= 8)
B <- subset(S, X1 == 3) #Given
Prob(A, given = B)
```

Any command-line input or output is written as follows:

```
docs[[1]]$content
```

New terms and **important words** are shown in bold. Words that you see on the screen, for example, in menus or dialog boxes, appear in the text like this: "Here is the step where you have to select **Advanced system settings**."

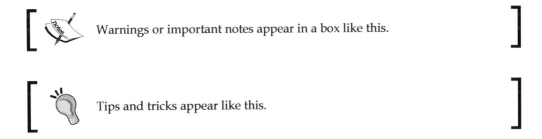

> Warnings or important notes appear in a box like this.

> Tips and tricks appear like this.

Reader feedback

Feedback from our readers is always welcome. Let us know what you think about this book—what you liked or disliked. Reader feedback is important for us as it helps us develop titles that you will really get the most out of.

To send us general feedback, simply e-mail feedback@packtpub.com, and mention the book's title in the subject of your message.

If there is a topic that you have expertise in and you are interested in either writing or contributing to a book, see our author guide at www.packtpub.com/authors.

Customer support

Now that you are the proud owner of a Packt book, we have a number of things to help you to get the most from your purchase.

Downloading the example code

You can download the example code files for this book from your account at http://www.packtpub.com. If you purchased this book elsewhere, you can visit http://www.packtpub.com/support and register to have the files e-mailed directly to you.

You can download the code files by following these steps:

1. Log in or register to our website using your e-mail address and password.
2. Hover the mouse pointer on the **SUPPORT** tab at the top.
3. Click on **Code Downloads & Errata**.
4. Enter the name of the book in the **Search** box.
5. Select the book for which you're looking to download the code files.
6. Choose from the drop-down menu where you purchased this book from.
7. Click on **Code Download**.

You can also download the code files by clicking on the **Code Files** button on the book's webpage at the Packt Publishing website. This page can be accessed by entering the book's name in the **Search** box. Please note that you need to be logged into your Packt account.

Once the file is downloaded, please make sure that you unzip or extract the folder using the latest version of:

- WinRAR / 7-Zip for Windows
- Zip eg / iZip / UnRarX for Mac
- 7-Zip / Pea Zip for Linux

The code bundle for the book is also hosted on GitHub at https://github.com/PacktPublishing/Mastering-Text-Mining-with-R. We also have other code bundles from our rich catalog of books and videos available at https://github.com/PacktPublishing/. Check them out!

Errata

Although we have taken every care to ensure the accuracy of our content, mistakes do happen. If you find a mistake in one of our books—maybe a mistake in the text or the code—we would be grateful if you could report this to us. By doing so, you can save other readers from frustration and help us improve subsequent versions of this book. If you find any errata, please report them by visiting http://www.packtpub.com/submit-errata, selecting your book, clicking on the **Errata Submission Form** link, and entering the details of your errata. Once your errata are verified, your submission will be accepted and the errata will be uploaded to our website or added to any list of existing errata under the Errata section of that title.

To view the previously submitted errata, go to https://www.packtpub.com/books/content/support and enter the name of the book in the search field. The required information will appear under the **Errata** section.

Piracy

Piracy of copyrighted material on the Internet is an ongoing problem across all media. At Packt, we take the protection of our copyright and licenses very seriously. If you come across any illegal copies of our works in any form on the Internet, please provide us with the location address or website name immediately so that we can pursue a remedy.

Please contact us at copyright@packtpub.com with a link to the suspected pirated material.

We appreciate your help in protecting our authors and our ability to bring you valuable content.

Questions

If you have a problem with any aspect of this book, you can contact us at questions@packtpub.com, and we will do our best to address the problem.

1

Statistical Linguistics with R

Statistics plays an important role in the fields that deal with quantitative data. Computational linguistics is no exception. The quantitative investigation of linguistic data helps us understand the latent patterns that have helped phoneticians, psycholinguistics, linguistics, and many others to explore and understand language.

In this chapter, we will explain the basic terms associated with probability, used in computational linguistics. You will soon get to dive into linguistics and learn about language models and practical quantitative methods used in linguistics.

At the end of this chapter, we will extensively discuss some very useful and highly efficient packages in R, which we will use throughout this book, and by the time you finish the book, you should be able to pick appropriate R packages and functions for specific text-mining activities and be able to effectively use them for practical purposes.

In this chapter, we will cover the following topics:

- Basic statistics and probability
- Probabilistic linguistics
- Language models
- Quantitative methods in linguistics
- R packages for text mining

Probability theory and basic statistics

The conceptual origin of statistics is perceived to be from probability theories. We all must have heard something like *the probability of rain tomorrow is 50%*. While this seems very quantitative and thus should be easily interpretable, it is not very clear what it means. It can be interpreted to mean that for all the days when weather conditions are the same as tomorrow, it will rain on half of those days.

Probability helps us calculate the extent to which something is likely to happen or the likelihood of an event.

Probability is useful in various fields, such as statistics, computer science, physics, finance, gambling, sports, medicine, and even in machine learning and artificial intelligence.

Probability space and event

Probability in mathematics is built around sets. Set theory is very useful in probability; it provides a language for expressing and working with events.

The sample space of an experiment is the set of all possible outcomes of the experiment; let's call it S. An event, let's call it **A,** is a subset of the sample space **S,** and we say that **A** occurred if the actual outcome is in **A**.

Let's take an example of picking a card from a standard deck of 52 cards. The sample space S is the set of all the cards. Let's us consider an event A where the card we pick is an ace. This is a subset of the sample space. So the probability P of picking an ace is:

Probability = (number of elements in the event) / (number of elements in the sample space).

Theorem of compound probabilities

This says that the probability of the intersection of two events A and B can be computed as the product of probability of A given that B has happened times the probability of B:

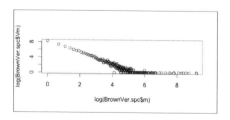

The law of total probability or law of alternatives can be formulated as follows:

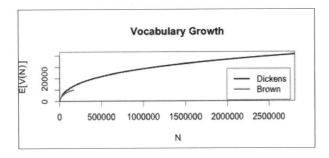

Conditional probability

Probability is a way of expressing uncertainties about events. Whenever we observe new evidence or obtain data, we acquire information that may affect our uncertainties. Conditional probability is the concept that tells us how to express the probability which is affected by the newly acquired information. Conditional probability handles situations where you have some additional knowledge about the outcome of a trial or experiment.

Let's consider an event R, *It will rain today*, before looking at the sky. The probability $P(R)$ will increase when we look at the sky and see dark clouds. So the new probability is $P(R \mid C)$ where C is the event of dark clouds.

If A and B are events with $P(B) > 0$, then the conditional probability of A given B, denoted by $P(A \mid B)$, is defined as:

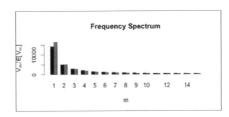

Let us consider an example and try to perform the same using R. We are rolling two dice and the objective is to find the probability of the sum of the outcomes being greater than or equal to 8, given that the first dice has resulted in 3:

```
library(prob)
S <- rolldie(2, makespace = TRUE)
A <- subset(S, X1 + X2 >= 8)
B <- subset(S, X1 == 3) #Given
Prob(A, given = B)
```

Bayes' formula for conditional probability

Bayes' formula gives us a way to test a hypothesis using conditional probabilities. A hypothesis is a suggested explanation for a specific outcome. If we see that a probability $P(A \mid B)$ is high, we might hypothesize that event B is a cause of the event A. We use Bayes' formula when we know conditional probabilities of the form $P(B \mid A)$ and want a conditional probability of the form $P(A \mid B)$:

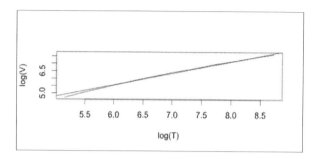

Independent events

Two events, A and B, in the same sample space are independent if $P(AB) = P(A) P(B)$. This formula gives us a new and simpler way to characterize independent events. Two events, A and B, are independent if the probability of both events happening together is equal to the product of the probabilities of the two events.

Random variables

In probability, a random variable is a rule or function that assigns a number to each element of a sample space. In other words, a random variable gives a number for each outcome of a random experiment. In statistics, we define random variables using the letter X. There are different types of random variable.

Discrete random variables

When we toss two coins, the number of heads we can get is 0, 1, or 2. We can define X as the number of heads that I get during this experiment. These random variable values have a probability associated with them; these variables can be represented as discrete points on a number line so they are called discrete random variables.

Continuous random variables

Let's say that we have to look at the physics test scores of 100 class 10 students. The test scores will fall between 0% and 100%. The test scores of the students may vary, such as 95.5%, 88%, 97.2%, and so on. We cannot denote all the test scores using discrete numbers when all values in an interval are possible. This is called a continuous random variable.

Probability frequency function

Once we have a random variable, we can determine the probability that the random variable will have a certain value; for example, for rolling two dice to get a sum of five outcomes, it can be (1,4) , (4,1) , (3,2) , or (2,3) so there are 4 out of 36 possible outcomes, so:

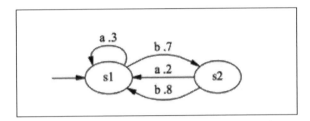

Probability distributions using R

R provides a wide range of probability functions. The generic prefixes for probability functions in R are r, d, p, q, for random number generators, probability density function, cumulative density function, and quantile function, respectively.

A comprehensive list of functions available is as follows:

Distribution	Functions			
Beta	pbeta	qbeta	dbeta	rbeta
Binomial	pbinom	qbinom	dbinom	rbinom
Cauchy	pcauchy	qcauchy	dcauchy	rcauchy
Chi-Square	pchisq	qchisq	dchisq	rchisq
Exponential	pexp	qexp	dexp	rexp
F	pf	qf	df	rf
Gamma	pgamma	qgamma	dgamma	rgamma
Geometric	pgeom	qgeom	dgeom	rgeom

Distribution	Functions			
Hypergeometric	phyper	qhyper	dhyper	rhyper
Logistic	plogis	qlogis	dlogis	rlogis
Log Normal	plnorm	qlnorm	dlnorm	rlnorm
Negative Binomial	pnbinom	qnbinom	dnbinom	rnbinom
Normal	pnorm	qnorm	dnorm	rnorm
Poisson	ppois	qpois	dpois	rpois
Student t	pt	qt	dt	rt
Studentized Range	ptukey	qtukey	dtukey	rtukey
Uniform	punif	qunif	dunif	runif
Weibull	pweibull	qweibull	dweibull	rweibull
Wilcoxon Rank Sum Statistic	pwilcox	qwilcox	dwilcox	rwilcox
Wilcoxon Signed Rank Statistic	psignrank	qsignrank	dsignrank	rsignrank

Cumulative distribution function

This frequency function gives the probabilities for each value in the range of a random variable. For a given value R of the random variable, the cumulative distribution function gives the probability of the random variable taking on a value up to and including the given value R. When R is 3, there are three outcomes, (1, 1), (1, 2), and (2, 1), so:

$$F(3) = \frac{3}{36} \approx \frac{3}{36}\frac{3}{36}\frac{3}{36} \approx 0.083$$

The cumulative distribution function is also called the CDF, or probability distribution or distribution function. The stats package in R provides the function `ecdf` to compute the empirical cumulative distribution function and plot it using the object created. You can also plot the `ecdf` object using the `ggplot2` package. Let's look at an example for the same:

```
x <- rnorm(1000, 99.2, 1.2)
y <- rnorm(10000, 97.3, 0.85)
```

```
z <- rnorm(10000, 98.1, 0.4)

# Create a chart with all 3 Conditional distribution plots
plot(ecdf(x), col=rgb(1,0,0), main=NA)
plot(ecdf(y), col=rgb(0,1,0), add=T)
plot(ecdf(z), col=rgb(0,0,1), add=T)

# Adding legend to the chart.
legend('right', c('x', 'y', 'z'), fill=c(rgb(1,0,0), rgb(0,1,0),
rgb(0,0,1)))
```

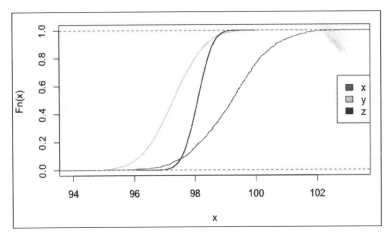

Using the ggplot2 package, create the CDF plot with the ecdf function:

```
# Load the required packages.
library("reshape2","plyr","ggplot2")

# transform the data.
plot_data <- melt(data.frame(x, y, z))
  plot_data <- ddply(plot_data, .(variable), transform, cd=ecdf(value)
(value))

# Create the CDF using ggplot.
  cdf <- ggplot(plot_data, aes(x=value)) + stat_
ecdf(aes(colour=variable))
```

```
# Generate the Conditional distribution plot.
cdf
```

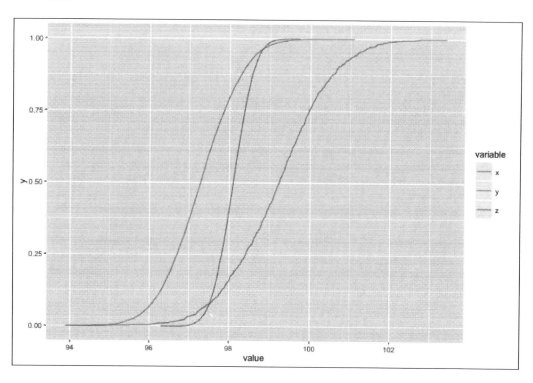

Joint distribution

Two different random variables can be associated with the same sample space. When there are two random variables on the same sample space, we study their interaction using a joint distribution. Let's consider an example: we want to know the probability that the sum of the same dice rolled twice is 6, so $S = 6$, and that the lowest die is 3, so $D = 3$. We represent this as follows:

P{S = 6, D = 3}

P {S = 6} = (1, 5) (2, 4) (3, 3) (4, 2) (1, 5);

Of the five outcomes, only one has the lower number equal to 3 so the probability is:

$$P\{X = 6, Y = 3\} = \frac{1}{36}\frac{1}{36}\frac{1}{36}\frac{1}{36}$$

Binomial distribution

If there are only two outcomes to a trial, one with probability P and the other with probability 1 – P, often one outcome is called a success and the other a failure. When this is the case, P is used as the probability of success and the probability of failure is 1 – P. Such an experiment is called a Bernoulli trial or a binomial trial, because there are only two outcomes. The random variable associated with a Bernoulli trial is the Bernoulli random variable, with value 1 for a successful outcome and value 0 for failure.

Let's take an example of flipping a coin. It gives two outcomes, heads and tails. If we assign the value 1 to heads and 0 to tails, we have a Bernoulli random variable. Let's call this random variable R and since heads and tails are equally likely to occur:

P{R = 1} = 0.5 and P{R = 0} = 0.5

If we repeat a Bernoulli trial many times over, we get a new distribution, called a **binomial distribution**. So in order to compute the probability of k successes in n trials we can use the following formula:

$$P\{X = k\} = nC_k \, P_k (1 - P)^{(n-k)}$$
$$P\{X = k\} = nC_k \, P_k (1 - P)^{(n-k)} (1 - P)(n - k)$$

Here:

- **n**: Number of trials
- **P**: Probability of success

Poisson distribution

The Poisson distribution applies when occurrences are independent, so that one occurrence neither diminishes nor increases the chance of another. The average frequency of occurrence for the time period is known. The probability of an occurrence during a small time interval is proportional to the entire length of the time interval:

$$P\{X = K\} = e^{-\lambda t} \, \frac{(\lambda t)^k}{k!}$$
$$\lambda P\{X = K\} = e^{-\lambda t} \, \frac{(\lambda t)^k}{k!}$$

Here:

- λ: Average rate of outcomes

- e≈ 2.71828

- t: Interval size

Counting occurrences

When we are putting together texts, we will not know the probability distribution of a particular topic. If we consider a corpus of country's economic strategy, written by various economists, it's difficult to understand the probability of what they are emphasizing more – is it infrastructure, manufacturing, banking, and so on – without counting the members associated. One thing to be aware of is no corpus will be balanced. We need to count the occurrences of relevant words in the dataset to get some statistical information. We need to know the frequency distribution of different words. Word frequencies refer to the number of word tokens that are instances of a word type. We can perform word counts over corpora with the **R tau** package.

Zipf's law

Zipf's law is an interesting phenomenon that can be applied universally in many contexts, such as social sciences, cognitive sciences, and linguistics. When we consider a variety of datasets, there will be an uneven distribution of words. Zipf's law says that the frequency of a word, $f(w)$, appears as a nonlinearly decreasing function of the rank of the word, $r(w)$, in a corpus. This law is a power law: the frequency is a function of the negative power of rank. C is a constant that is determined by the particulars of the corpus; it's the frequency of the most frequent word:

$$f(w) = \frac{C}{r(w)^a}$$
$$f(w) = \frac{C}{r(w)^a}$$

Given a collection of words, we can estimate the frequency of each unique word, which is nothing but the number of times the word occurs in the collection.

If we sort the words in descending order of their frequency of occurrence in the collection, and compute their rank, the product of their frequency and associated rank reveals a very interesting pattern.

- **N**: Sample size or corpus size
- **V**: Vocabulary size, count of distinct type in the corpus
- **Vm**: Count of hapax terms, types that occur just once in a corpus

Let us consider a small sample **S**: a a a a b b b c c d d:

1. Here, *N= 11, V = 4, Vm = 0*.
2. Load Brown and Dickens frequency data:

```
library(zipfR)
data(Dickens.spc)
data(BrownVer.spc)
```

3. Check sample size and vocabulary and hapax counts:

```
N(BrownVer.spc)        # 166262
V(BrownVer.spc)        # 10007
Vm(BrownVer.spc,1)     # 3787
N(Dickens.spc)         # 2817208
V(Dickens.spc)         # 41116
Vm(Dickens.spc,1)      # 14220
```

4. Zipf rank-frequency plot:

```
plot(log(BrownVer.spc$m),log(BrownVer.spc$Vm))
```

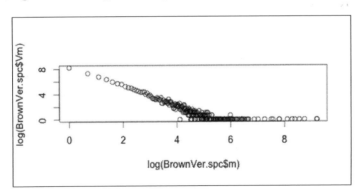

5. Compute binomially interpolated growth curves:

```
di.vgc <- vgc.interp(Dickens.spc,(1:100)*28170)
br.vgc <- vgc.interp(BrownVer.spc,(1:100)*1662)
```

6. Plot vocabulary growth:

```
plot(di.vgc,br.vgc,legend=c("Dickens","Brown"))
```

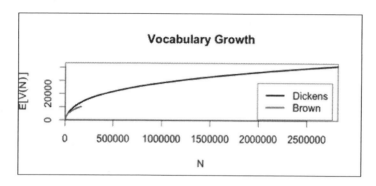

7. Compute Zipf-Mandelbrot model from Dickens data:

```
zm <- lnre("zm",Dickens.spc)
## plot observed and expected spectrum
zm.spc <- lnre.spc(zm,N(Dickens.spc))
```

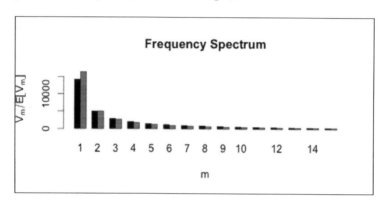

Let there be a word w which has the rank r' in a document and the probability of this word to be at rank r' be defined as $P(r')$. The probability $P(r')$ can be expressed as the function of frequency of occurrence of the words as follows:

```
P(r') = Freq(r')/N,
```

where N is the sample size and $Freq(r')$ is the frequency of occurrence of r' in the corpus

 As per Zipf's law, $r' * P(r') = K$, where K is a constant. The value of K is assumed to be close to 0.1.

Heaps' law

Heaps' law is also known as Herdan's Law. This law was discovered by Gustav Herdan, but the law is sometimes attributed to Harold Heaps. It is an empirical law which describes the relationship between type and tokens in linguistics. In simpler terms, Heaps' law defines the relation between the count of distinct words in document and the length of the specified document.

The relation can be expressed as:

Vr(n) = C* nb

Here, Vr is the count of distinct words in document and n is the size of the document. C and b are parameters defined empirically.

The similarity between Heaps' Law and Zipf's law is attributed to the fact that type-token relation is derivable from type distribution:

```
library(tm)
data("acq")
termdoc <- DocumentTermMatrix(acq)
Heaps_plot(termdoc)
```

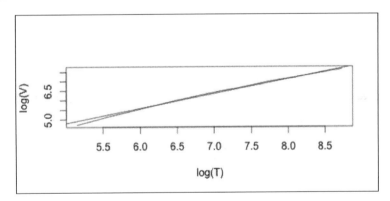

Lexical richness

Quantitative analysis of lexical structure is relevant for many activities such as stylometrics, applied linguistics, computational linguistics, natural language processing, lexicology, and so on. There are different approaches to capture vocabulary richness. It can be measured by means of measure or of an index. It can be captured by means of curve, as in the case of Herdan's and Zipf's law. If we consider the empirical distribution of word types, we can derive the distribution based on combinatorial considerations or we can use consider the stochastic processes to derive the distribution.

In applied linguistics, lexical richness explains the qualified proficiency of the author in a document, in terms of language variation, width, length, and productive knowledge of vocabulary. Let's attempt to understand the multiple measures that explain the lexical richness of a text.

 The **languageR** package in R comes with functions to compare lexical richness between corpora.

Lexical variation

Lexical variation in language is considered to be multi-dimensional; all languages go through variations based on time and social settings. There are different lexical variants to the same word in same language. For instance, in the US, what you call a **cookie** is a **biscuit** in the UK. Most of us are aware of language variation based on geographical differences, such as elevator and lift, pavement and sidewalk, pants and trousers. Socio-cultural changes lead to the phenomenon of borrowing in cases of dialect contacts. Semantic shifts and broadening give the words different meanings in different contexts. While by semantic broadening, the words take a more generalized meaning, by semantic narrowing, it is bound to take more restricted meaning. Broadly, lexical variations are of two categories: conceptual variation and contextual variation, which is further categorized to formal variation, semasiologically variation, and onomasiolofical variation.

 The *koRpus* package in R provides functions to estimate lexical variation.

Lexical density

Lexical density is defined as the ratio of content to functional or grammatical words in a sentence. It is used in discourse analysis for texts. In simpler terms, lexical density explains the readability of a text.

Lexical density is determined as follows:

```
Ld  = (Nlex / N) * 100
```

Here:

- Ld = Lexical density
- Nlex = Count of lexical tokens
- N = Count of all tokens

Lexical originality

Lexical originality measures the unique wording of a specific writer. It is defined as the *number of unique word types*100/total lexical words.*

Lexical sophistication

Lexical sophistication measures the percentage of advanced words in text. It is defined as the *(number of advanced lexemes)*100 /(total number of lexical words).*

For identifying single word lexemes, we can use the technique of stemming.

Language models

In terms of natural language processing, language models generate output strings that help to assess the likelihood of a bunch of strings to be a sentence in a specific language. If we discard the sequence of words in all sentences of a text corpus and basically treat it like a bag of words, then the efficiency of different language models can be estimated by how accurately a model restored the order of strings in sentences. Which sentence is more likely: *I am learning text mining* or *I text mining learning am*? Which word is more likely to follow *I am…*?

Language models are widely used in machine translation, spelling correction, speech recognition, text summarization, questionnaires, and so on.

Basically, a language model assigns the probability of a sentence being in a correct order. The probability is assigned over the sequence of terms by using conditional probability. Let us define a simple language modeling problem. Assume a bag of words contains words *W1, W2,.....................,Wn..* A language model can be defined to compute any of the following:

- Estimate the probability of a sentence S1: *P (S1) = P (W1, W2, W3, W4, W5)*
- Estimate the probability of the next word in a sentence or set of strings:

```
P (W3|W2, W1)
```

How to compute the probability? We will use chain law, by decomposing the sentence probability as a product of smaller string probabilities:

```
P(W1W2W3W4) = P(W1)P(W2|W1)P(W3|W1W2)P(W4|W1W2W3)
```

N-gram models

N-grams are important for a wide range of applications. They can be used to build simple language models. Let's consider a text T with W tokens. Let SW be a sliding window. If the sliding window consists of one cell ($w_i w_i w_i w_i$) then the collection of strings is called a unigram; if the sliding window consists of two cells, the output is $(w_1, w_2)(w_3, w_4)(w_5 w_5, w_5)(w_1, w_2)(w_3, w_4)(w_5, w_5)$, this is called a bigram .Using conditional probability, we can define the probability of a word having seen the previous word; this is known as bigram probability. So the conditional probability of an element, , given the previous element, (w_i-1) is:

$$P(w_i|w_{i-1})$$

Extending the sliding window, we can generalize that n-gram probability as the conditional probability of an element given previous n-1 element:

$$P(w_i|w_{i-n-1} \ldots w_{i-1})$$

The most common bigrams in any corpus are not very interesting, such as *on the*, *can be, in it, it is*. In order to get more meaningful bigrams, we can run the corpus through a **part-of-speech (POS)** tagger. This would filter the bigrams to more content-related pairs such as *infrastructure development, agricultural subsidies, banking rates*; this can be one way of filtering less meaningful bigrams.

A better way to approach this problem is to take into account **collocations**; a collocation is the string created when two or more words co-occur in a language more frequently. One way to do this over a corpus is **pointwise mutual information (PMI)**. The concept behind PMI is for two words, A and B, we would like to know how much one word tells us about the other. For example, given an occurrence of A, a, and an occurrence of B, b, how much does their joint probability differ from the expected value of assuming that they are independent. This can be expressed as follows:

$$PMI(a, b) = \ln \frac{P(a,b)}{P(a)P(b)} \quad PMI(a, b) = \ln \frac{P(a,b)}{P(a)P(b)}$$

- Unigram model:

$$\text{Punigram(W1W2W3W4)} = \text{P(W1)P(W2)P(W3)P(W4)}$$

- Bigram model:

$$\text{Pbu(W1W2W3W4)} = \text{P(W1)P(W2|W1)P(W3|W2)P(W4|W3)}$$
$$\text{P(w1w2...wn)} = \text{P(wi | w1w2...wi"1)}$$

Applying the chain rule on n contexts can be difficult to estimate; Markov assumption is applied to handle such situations.

Markov assumption

If predicting that a current string is independent of some word string in the past, we can drop that string to simplify the probability. Say the history consists of three words, Wi, Wi-1, Wi-2, instead of estimating the probability P(Wi+1) using P(Wi,i-1,i-2) , we can directly apply P(Wi+1 | Wi, Wi-1).

Hidden Markov models

Markov chains are used to study systems that are subject to random influences. Markov chains model systems that move from one state to another in steps governed by probabilities. The same set of outcomes in a sequence of trials is called states. Knowing the probabilities of states is called **state distribution**. The state distribution in which the system starts is the initial state distribution. The probability of going from one state to another is called transition probability. A Markov chain consists of a collection of states along with transition probabilities. The study of Markov chains is useful to understand the long-term behavior of a system. Each arc associates to certain probability value and all arcs coming out of each node must have exhibit a probability distribution. In simple terms, there is a probability associated to every transition in states:

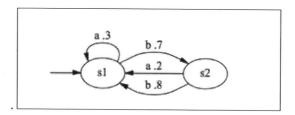

Hidden Markov models are non-deterministic Markov chains. They are an extension of Markov models in which output symbol is not the same as state. We will discuss this topic in detail in later chapters.

Quantitative methods in linguistics

Text can be grammatically complex, to analyze text its difficult consider all the complexity. In order to get meaning out of text or a document, we need a measure. We need to extract quantitative data by processing the text with various transformation methods. Each method discards unnecessary, ancillary information. There are various methods, packages, APIs, and software that can transform text into quantitative data, but before using any of them, we need to analyze and test our documents with different approaches.

The first step is we assume a document is a collection of words where order doesn't influence our analysis. We consider unigrams; for some analysis, bigrams and trigrams can also be used to provide more meaningful results. Next, we simplify the vocabulary by passing the document through a stemming process; here, we reduce the words to their root. A better/advanced approach would be lemmatization. Then we discard punctuation, capitalization, stop words, and very common words. Now we use this text for quantitative analysis. Let me list a few quantity methods and explain why they are used.

Document term matrix

In order to find the similarity between documents in a corpus, we can use a document term matrix. In a document term matrix, rows represent documents, columns represent terms, and each cell value is the term frequency count for a document. It is one of the useful ways of modeling documents. Here is an example:

- **Document-1**: Ice creams in summer are awesome
- **Document-2**: I love ice creams in summer
- **Document-3**: Ice creams are awesome all season

	icecream	summer	love	awesome	season
Doc1	1	1	0	1	0
Doc2	1	1	1	0	0
Doc3	1	0	0	1	1

If we visualize this in a term-document space, each document becomes a point in it. We can then tell how similar two documents are by calculating the distance between the two points using Euclidean distance.

When a term occurs in a lot of documents, it tends to make notably less difference the terms that occur few times. For example, *India Today* has more to do with *India* than *today*. These frequently occurring terms can affect the similarity comparison. The term space will be biased towards these terms. In order to address this problem, we use inverse document frequency.

Inverse document frequency

A commonly used measure of a term's selective potential is calculated by its **inverse document frequency (IDF)**. The formula for IDF is calculated as follows:

$$idf(term) = log \frac{N}{df(term)}$$

$$idf(term) = log \frac{N}{df(term)}$$

Here, N is the number of documents in the `corpus` and `df(term)` is the number of documents in which the term appears.

The weight of a term's appearance in a document is calculated by combining the **term frequency** (TF) in the document with its IDF:

$$w(t, d) = tfd(t) * idf(t)$$
$$w(t, d) = tfd(t) * idf(t)$$

This term–document score is known as **TF*IDF**, and is widely used. This is used by a lot of search platforms/APIs, such as SOLR, Elasticsearch, and lucene. TF*IDF scores are then pre-computed and stored, so that similarity comparison can be done by just a dot product.

When we look at the entries in this term–document matrix, most of the cells will be empty because only a few terms appear in each document; storing all the empty cells requires a lot of memory and it contributes no value to the dot product (similarity computation). Various *sparse matrix* representations are possible and these are used to for optimized query processing.

Words similarity and edit-distance functions

In order to find a similarity between words in case of fuzzy searches, we need to quantify the similarity between words; some quantitative methods used are explained below. Before going into it, let's install an R package, `stringdist`, which can be used to apply various algorithms mentioned above to calculate string similarity:

```
install.packages("stringdist")
library(stringdist)
```

One way of finding the similarity between two words is by edit distance. Edit distance refers to the number of operations required to transform one string into another.

Euclidean distance

Euclidean distance is the distance between two points in the term-document space; it can be calculated by using the formula for a two-dimensional space as follows:

```
Euclidean distance e <- sqrt((x1-x2)^2+(y1-y2)^2)
```

Here, *(x1,y1)* and *(x2,y2)* are the two points and *e* is the estimated Euclidean distance between them:

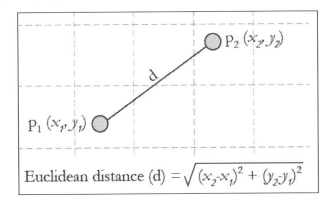

$$\text{Euclidean distance (d)} = \sqrt{(x_2\text{-}x_1)^2 + (y_2\text{-}y_1)^2}$$

We can very easily convert the aforesaid formula into R code:

```
euclidean.dist <- function(x1, x2) sqrt(sum((x1 - x2) ^ 2))
```

Cosine similarity

Euclidean distance has its own pitfalls, documents with lots of terms are far from origin, we will find small documents relatively similar even if it's unrelated because of short distance.

To avoid length issues, we can use the angular distance and measure the similarity by the angle between the vectors; we measure the cosine of the angle. The larger the cosine value, the more similar the documents are. Since we use the cos function, this is also called cosine similarity:

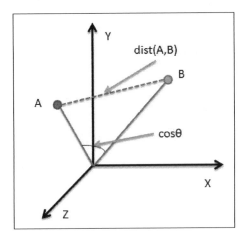

The formula to calculate cosine between two points is as follows:

$$\cos(A, B) = \frac{A.B}{|A|.|B|}$$

$$\cos(A, B) = \frac{A.B}{|A|.|B|}$$

This kind of geometric modeling is also called vector space model:

```
# Create two random matrices matrixA and matrixB
ncol<-5
nrow<-5
matrixA<-matrix(runif(ncol*nrow), ncol=ncol)
matrixB<-matrix(runif(ncol*nrow), ncol=ncol)

# function for estimating cosine similarity in R:
cosine_sim<-function(matrixA, matrixB){
  m=tcrossprod(matrixA, matrixB)
  c1=sqrt(apply(matrixA, 1, crossprod))
  c2=sqrt(apply(matrixB, 1, crossprod))
  m / outer(c1,c2)
}

# Estimate the cosine similarity between the two matrices initiated
earlier
cosine_sim(matrixA,matrixB)
```

Alternately, cosine similarity can also be estimated by functions available in the packages lsa, proxy, and so on.

Levenshtein distance

The Levenshtein distance between two words, x and y, is the minimal number of insertions, deletions, and replacements needed for transforming word x into word y.

If we to convert *abcd* to *abdc*, we need to replace c with d and replace d with c so the distance is 2:

```
Library(stringdist)
stringdist('abcd', 'abdc', method='lv')
     [1] 2
```

Damerau-Levenshtein distance

The Damerau-Levenshtein distance is the minimal number of insertions, deletions, replacements, and adjacent transpositions needed for transforming word *x* into word *y*.

If we to convert *abcd* to *abdc*, we need to swap c and d so the distance is 1:

```
stringdist('abcd', 'abdc', method='dl')
     [1] 1
```

Hamming distance

The Hamming distance between two words is the number of positions at which the characters are different. It is the minimum number of substitutions required to change into word into another. In order to use the Hamming distance, the words must be of the same length.

If we to convert *abcd* to *abdc*, we need to substitute c with d and d with c so the distance is 2:

```
stringdist('abcd', 'abdc', method='hamming')
     [1] 2
```

Jaro-Winkler distance

The Jaro-Winkler distance measure is best suited for short strings such as name comparison or record linkage. It is designed to compare surnames and names. The higher the distance, the more similar the strings in comparison are.

In order to measure the Jaro distance, we need to perform the following two tasks:

- Compute the number of matches
- Compute the number of transpositions

The Winkler adjustment involves a final rescoring based on an exact match score for the initial characters of both words. It uses a constant scaling factor P:

```
stringdist('abcd', 'abdc' , method = 'jw' , p=0.1)
     [1] 0.06666667
```

Measuring readability of a text

Readability is the ease with which a text can be read by a reader. The readability of a text depends on its content and the complexity of its vocabulary and syntax. There are a number of methods to measure the readability of a text. Most of them are based on correlation analysis, where researchers have selected a number of text properties (such as words per sentence, average number of syllables per word, and so on) and then asked test subjects to grade the readability of various texts on a scale. By looking at the text properties of these texts, it is possible to correlate how much "words per sentence" influences readability.

 The koRpus package in R provides a hyphen function to estimate the readability of a given text.

Gunning frog index

The Gunning fog index is one of the best-known methods that measure the level of reading difficulty of any document. The fog index level translates the number of years of education a reader needs in order to understand the given material. The ideal score is 7 or 8; anything above 12 is too hard for most people to read.

The Gunning fog index is calculated as shown in the following steps:

1. Select all the sentences in a passage of approximately 100 words.
2. We need to calculate the average sentence length by doing a simple math of dividing number of words by number of sentences.
3. Count all the words with three or more syllables. Generally, words with more than three syllables are considered to be complex.
4. Sum up the average sentence length and the percentage of complex words.
5. Multiply the result by 0.4.

    The formula is as shown here:

$$0.4[(\frac{words}{sentences}) + 100(\frac{complex\ words}{words})]$$

$$0.4[(\frac{words}{sentences}) + 100(\frac{complex\ words}{words})]$$

R packages for text mining

There is a wide range of packages available in R for natural language processing. Some of them are as follows.

OpenNLP

OpenNLP is an R package which provides an interface, Apache OpenNLP, which is a machine-learning-based toolkit written in Java for natural language processing activities. Apache OpenNLP is widely used for most common tasks in NLP, such as tokenization, POS tagging, **named entity recognition** (**NER**), chunking, parsing, and so on. It provides wrappers for Maxent entropy models using the Maxent Java package.

It provides functions for sentence annotation, word annotation, POS tag annotation, and annotation parsing using the Apache OpenNLP chunking parser. The Maxent Chunk annotator function computes the chunk annotation using the Maxent chunker provided by OpenNLP.

The Maxent entity annotator function in R package utilizes the Apache OpenNLP Maxent name finder for entity annotation. Model files can be downloaded from `http://opennlp.sourceforge.net/models-1.5/`. These language models can be effectively used in R packages by installing the OpenNLPmodels.language package from the repository at `http://datacube.wu.ac.at`.

Rweka

The RWeka package in R provides an interface to Weka. Weka is an open source software developed by a machine learning group at the University of Wakaito, which provides a wide range of machine learning algorithms which can either be directly applied to a dataset or it can be called from a Java code. Different data-mining activities, such as data processing, supervised and unsupervised learning, association mining, and so on, can be performed using the RWeka package. For natural language processing, RWeka provides tokenization and stemming functions. RWeka packages provide an interface to Alphabetic, NGramTokenizers, and wordTokenizer functions, which can efficiently perform tokenization for contiguous alphabetic sequence, string-split to n-grams, or simple word tokenization, respectively.

RcmdrPlugin.temis

The `RcmdrPlugin.temis` package in R provides a graphical integrated text-mining solution. This package can be leveraged for many text-mining tasks, such as importing and cleaning a corpus, terms and documents count, term co-occurrences, correspondence analysis, and so on. Corpora can be imported from different sources and analysed using the `importCorpusDlg` function. The package provides flexible data source options to import corpora from different sources, such as text files, spreadsheet files, XML, HTML files, Alceste format and Twitter search. The Import function in this package processes the corpus and generates a term-document matrix. The package provides different functions to summarize and visualize the corpus statistics. Correspondence analysis and hierarchical clustering can be performed on the corpus. The `corpusDissimilarity` function helps analyse and create a cross-dissimilarity table between term-documents present in the corpus.

This package provides many functions to help the users explore the corpus. For example, `frequentTerms` to list the most frequent terms of a corpus, `specificTerms` to list terms most associated with each document, `subsetCorpusByTermsDlg` to create a subset of the corpus. Term frequency, term co-occurrence, term dictionary, temporal evolution of occurrences or term time series, term metadata variables, and corpus temporal evolution are among the other very useful functions available in this package for text mining.

tm

The tm package is a text-mining framework which provides some powerful functions which will aid in text-processing steps. It has methods for importing data, handling corpus, metadata management, creation of term document matrices, and preprocessing methods. For managing documents using the tm package, we create a corpus which is a collection of text documents. There are two types of implementation, volatile corpus (VCorpus) and permanent corpus (PCropus). VCorpus is completely held in memory and when the R object is destroyed the corpus is gone. PCropus is stored in the filesystem and is present even after the R object is destroyed; this corpus can be created by using the VCorpus and PCorpus functions respectively. This package provides a few predefined sources which can be used to import text, such as DirSource, VectorSource, or DataframeSource. The getSources method lists available sources, and users can create their own sources. The tm package ships with several reader options: readPlain, readPDF, and readDOC. We can execute the getReaders method for an up-to-date list of available readers. To write a corpus to the filesystem, we can use writeCorpus.

For inspecting a corpus, there are methods such as inspect and print. For transformation of text, such as stop-word removal, stemming, whitespace removal, and so on, we can use the `tm_map`, `content_transformer`, `tolower`, `stopwords("english")` functions. For metadata management, meta comes in handy. The tm package provides various quantitative function for text analysis, such as DocumentTermMatrix , findFreqTerms, findAssocs, and removeSparseTerms.

languageR

`languageR` provides datasets and functions for statistical analysis on text data. This package contains functions for vocabulary richness, vocabulary growth, frequency spectrum, also mixed-effects models and so on. There are simulation functions available: simple regression, quasi-F factor, and Latin-square designs. Apart from that, this package can also be used for correlation, collinearity diagnostic, diagnostic visualization of logistic models, and so on.

koRpus

The koRpus package is a versatile tool for text mining which implements many functions for text readability and lexical variation. Apart from that, it can also be used for basic level functions such as tokenization and POS tagging.

RKEA

The RKEA package provides an interface to KEA, which is a tool for keyword extraction from texts. RKEA requires a keyword extraction model, which can be created by manually indexing a small set of texts, using which it extracts keywords from the document.

maxent

The maxent package in R provides tools for low-memory implementation of multinomial logistic regression, which is also called the maximum entropy model. This package is quite helpful for classification processes involving sparse term-document matrices, and low memory consumption on huge datasets.

lsa

Truncated singular vector decomposition can help overcome the variability in a term-document matrix by deriving the latent features statistically. The lsa package in R provides an implementation of latent semantic analysis.

Summary

Text mining is an interdisciplinary field which involves modelling unstructured data to extract information and knowledge, leveraging numerous statistical, machine learning, and computational linguistic techniques. The text analysis process involves multiple steps, which we will describe in upcoming chapters with practical examples using R. Any data analysis process starts with a preliminary step that comprises data preprocessing and cleansing, and exploratory analysis of the data. In this chapter, we focused on familiarizing you with the important NLP terminologies that will be frequently used throughout this book; this chapter can also act as a quick reference to the NLP packages in R and their widespread utility in different text-mining tasks. The next chapter deals with basic to advanced-level text-processing techniques to empower you with tools and techniques to process unstructured data efficiently.

2
Processing Text

A significant part of the time spent on any modeling or analysis activity goes into accessing, preprocessing, and cleaning the data. We should have the capability to access data from diverse sources, load them in our statistical analysis environment and process them in a manner conducive for advanced analysis.

In this chapter, we will learn to access data from a wide variety of sources and load it into our R environment. We will also learn to perform some standard text processing.

By the time you finish the chapter, you should be equipped with enough knowledge to retrieve data from most of the data sources and process it into custom corpus for further analysis:

- Accessing texts from diverse sources
- Processing texts using regular expressions
- Normalizing texts
- Lexical diversity
- Language detection

Accessing text from diverse sources

Reading data from diverse sources for analysis, and exporting the results to another system for reporting purposes can be a daunting task that can sometimes take even more time than the real analysis. There are various sources from which we can gather text; some of them are HTML pages, social media, RSS feeds, JSON or XML, enterprise environments, and so on. The source has a very important role to play in the quality of textual data and the way we access the source. For instance, in the case of an enterprise environment, the common sources of text or data can be database and log files. In a web ecosystem, web pages are the source of data. When we consider web service applications, the sources can be JSON or XML over HTTP or HTTPS. We will look into various data sources and ways in which we can collect data from them.

File system

Reading from a file system is a very basic capability that any programming language should provide. We may have collections of documents on our file systems all stored in a folder, but in order to work on these files we need the capability to load them into our statistical analysis environment. The files may be in different formats like .doc, .txt, .pdf, .csv, and .xml. The tm package in R provides a framework to access and perform a wide variety of analysis on text.

In order to execute the following R functions, first we need to load package tm. We will use the following command to install and load the package:

```
install.packages("tm")

library(tm)
```

PDF documents

If we need to load corpus of PDF documents then we can use the readPDF() reader function to convert PDF into text and have that loaded as our corpus.

In order to read the PDF file we need to install xpdf. Download the precompiled binaries based on your operating system from http://www.foolabs.com/xpdf/. Once the zip file is downloaded, unzip it to any folder of your choice. We must add the binaries to the system path:

1. In a windows system you can go to **My Computer** | **Properties** (right click on it) | **Advance system settings** | **Advance** | **Environment variables** | **System variables** path provide the downloaded location D:/R/Chapter_2/corpus/pdf/xpdfbin-win-3.04/xpdfbin-win-3.04/bin64/ and click on **OK**.

2. You can refer to the following screenshots:

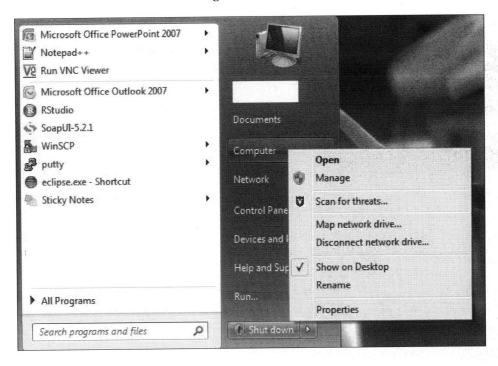

3. Here is the step where you have to select **Advanced system settings**:

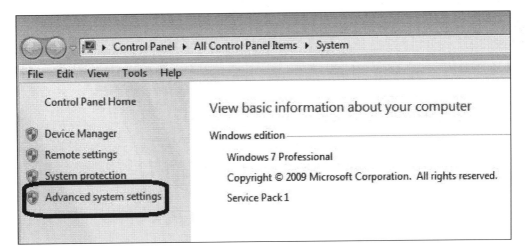

4. The next step is as shown in following screenshot:

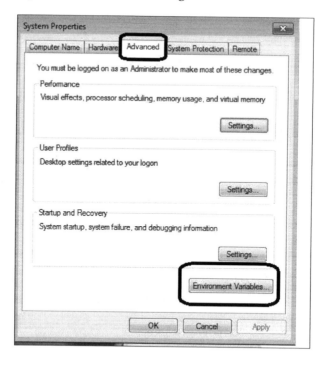

5. Then, you have to provide the path as shown in the following screenshot:

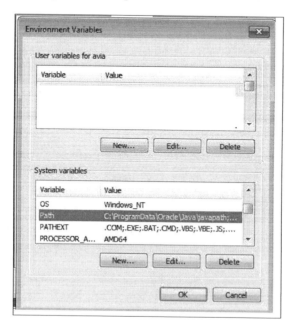

6. The path is as shown in the following code:

```
system("D:/R/Chapter_2/corpus/pdf/xpdfbin-win-3.04/xpdfbin-
win-3.04/bin64/pdftotext.exe", wait=FALSE)
system("D:/R/Chapter_2/corpus/pdf/xpdfbin-win-3.04/xpdfbin-
win-3.04/bin64/pdfinfo.exe", wait=FALSE)
```

7. The folder where the PDF is located is as shown in the following code:

```
pathToPdf <- "D:/R/Chapter_2/corpus/pdf/testFile/"

docs <- Corpus(DirSource(pathToPdf), readerControl =
list(reader=readPDF))
```

8. Ignore any warnings you may get.

9. Let's check the content loaded from the PDF file:

```
docs[[1]]$content
```

```
[1] "This is a test PDF for learning text mining." ""
```

10. This will use, by default, the `pdftotext` command from `xpdf` to convert the PDF into text format. The `xpdf` application needs to be installed for `readPDF()` to word.

Microsoft Word documents

We can use the `readDOC()` reader function to convert Microsoft Word documents into text and have that loaded as corpus. `readDOC` requires the `antiword` application to be installed; once it is available it can be utilized by `tm` to convert Word documents into text for loading into R.

In order to read the `doc` file we need to install a third party tool `antiword` - download the `zip` file from `http://www.winfield.demon.nl/` based on your operating system.

Once the `zip` file is downloaded, unzip it to any folder of your choice. We must add the binaries to system path. You can follow the same procedure as mentioned in the reading PDF section path to the document location as shown in the following code:

```
pathToDoc <- "D:/R/Chapter_2/corpus/worddoc/test/"# set the
antiword.exe to system path

system("D:/R/Chapter_2/corpus/worddoc/antiword/antiword.exe",
wait=FALSE)
```

To check on which path the `antiword` is installed, refer the following command:

```
flag <- Sys.which("antiword")
```

Read the following document:

```
docs <- Corpus(DirSource(pathToDoc), readerControl =
list(reader=readDOC))
```

Sometimes we might get error as follows, a simple hack is to copy the mapping file in to the required folder:

```
> docs <- Corpus(DirSource(pathToDoc), readerControl = list(reader=readDOC()))
Warning message:
running command '"antiword"  "D:\R\Chapter_2\corpus\worddoc\test\TestDoc.doc"' had status 1
> docs[[1]]$content
 [1] "I can't open your mapping file (8859-1.txt)"
 [2] "It is not in 'C:/Users/avia.ORADEV/Documents\\antiword' nor in 'C:\\antiword'."
 [3] "\tName: antiword.exe"
 [4] "\tPurpose: Display MS-Word files"
 [5] "\tAuthor: (C) 1998-2005 Adri van Os"
 [6] "\tVersion: 0.37  (21 Oct 2005)"
 [7] "\tStatus: GNU General Public License"
 [8] "\tUsage: antiword.exe [switches] wordfile1 [wordfile2 ...]"
 [9] "\tSwitches: [-f|-t|-a papersize|-p papersize|-x dtd][-m mapping][-w #][-i #][-Ls]"
[10] "\t\t-f formatted text output"
```

We created a folder `antiword` in `C:\Users\Documents\"` copied the mapping text `8859-1.txt` to this path.

Execute the following command:

```
docs[[1]]$content
```

After executing the program, we will get the following output:

```
> docs <- Corpus(DirSource(pathToDoc), readerControl = list(reader=readDOC()))
> docs[[1]]$content
[1] ""                        "Let us learn text mining." ""
>
```

The `antiword` program takes some useful command line arguments. We can pass these through to the program from `readDOC()` by specifying them as the character string argument here, `-r` requests that removed text be included in the output, and `-s` requests that text hidden by Word be included.

```
docs <- Corpus(DirSource(pathToDoc),
readerControl=list(reader=readDOC("-r -s")))
```

Similarly there are various readers such as `readPlain()` for text files and, `readXML()` from `xml` files.

HTML

Hyper Text Markup Language (HTML) is the standard language behind everything we see while surfing the web, searching on Google, being social on Facebook or Twitter or, looking for information on Wikipedia. When we use browsers like Firefox or, Chrome, we use HTML which the browser interprets.

There are syntax rules that an HTML document or page has to adhere to, in order to be rendered properly on the browser, and there are list of elements and tags available with various attributes to create an HTML page. Having a basic understanding of the DOM structuring and CSS will aid in parsing the web pages to extract relevant information.

Parsing is an important step in processing information from web documents. We need to parse an HTML document in order to extract relevant information. The structure of HTML does not naturally map into R objects. We can import HTML files as raw text, but this deprives us of the most useful features of these documents:

```
install.packages("RCurl")
install.packages("XML")
install.packages("selectr")
library(RCurl)
library(XML)
library(selectr)
```

Let's access the following URL, and print `First Name` column from the HTML table (refer to the example):

```
URL <- "http://www.w3schools.com/html/html_tables.asp"
```

The `getURL` retrieves the content from the specified URL. This function is from the RCurl package:

```
webpage <- getURL(URL)
```

We can use `htmlParse()` or `htmlTreeParse()` to correct not well-formed docs by using heuristics that will take care of the missing elements. This function is from XML package:

```
pagetree <- htmlTreeParse(webpage, error=function(...){},
useInternalNodes = TRUE)
```

We can use `querySelector()` to select elements from an HTML document. This function is from selector package:

```
table <- querySelector(pagetree, '.reference')
```

This function get all the nodes matching the `xpath`:

```
name <- xpathApply(table, "./tr/td[2]")

 print (name)
```

This function gets all the nodes matching the `xpath` and applies `SApply` function on it to get only the value of the nodes and to filter out `td`:

```
textVal <- xpathSApply(table, "./tr/td[2]", xmlValue)
```

```
print(textVal)
```

There are a myriad of functions in `XML`, and `RCurl`, `selectr` packages that will help in cleansing, accessing text from XML and HTML documents, and going through the package documentations to use appropriate functions. Understanding `xpath` is very useful as it's a powerful tool to access data from specific elements.

There are event driven or Simple API for XML (SAX) style parsers which process XML without building the tree, but rather identify tokens in the stream of characters and pass them to handlers, which can extract only relevant data and consume less memory.

XML

Extensible Markup Language (XML) is one of the most popular formats for exchanging data over the web. XML has been the syntax of choice for designing document formats across almost all computer applications. XML is robust, reliable, and has flexible document syntax. The main purpose of XML is to store data. It is a hardware or software agnostic method of data exchange between computer applications.

XML has syntax rules; values and names are wrapped in meaningful tags and it has a hierarchical structure. We will learn how to import XML data into R and how to transform it into other data formats that are more convenient for analysis.

Let's see some basic syntax rules that will help in parsing:

- An XML document must have a root element
- All elements must have a start tag and be closed, except for the declaration, which is not part of the actual XML document
- XML elements must be properly nested

- XML attribute values must be quoted
- Tags are named with characters and numbers, but may not start with a number or XML
- Tag names may not contain spaces and are case sensitive
- Space characters are preserved
- Some characters are illegal and have to be replaced by meta characters
- Comments can be included as follows:

  ```
  <!-- comment -->
  ```

The `xmlParse()` function is used to parse the XML document. The parsing function provides a set of options to decide whether both namespace URI and prefix should be provided, to determine whether an XML schema is parsed or to validate the XML against XSD:

```
library(XML)
parsed_catelogue <- xmlParse(file ="D:/R/Chapter_2/simple.xml")
class(parsed_catalogue)
root <- xmlRoot(parsed_catalogue)
class(root)
```

Once we have this representation we can perform operations on the object get root element name:

```
xmlName(root)
```

get number of elements in root element:

```
xmlSize(root)
```

We can use numerical or named indices to select certain nodes. This is not possible with objects of class XMLInternalDocument that are generated by xmlParse(). We therefore work with the root object, which belongs to the class XMLInternalElementNode:

- Prints the 1st child:

  ```
  root[1]
  ```

- Prints 1st childs 1st child:

  ```
  root[[1]][[1]]
  ```

- Element names can also be used to navigate through the document:

  ```
  root[["book"]][[1]][[1]]
  ```

Sometimes it suffices to transform an entire XML object into R data structures like vectors, data frames, or lists. We can use methods like `xmlSApply()` in conjunction with `xmlValue()` and `xmlGetAttr()` to do this:

```
xmlSApply(root[["book"]],xmlValue)
```

```
xmlSApply(root,xmlGetAttr,"id")
```

For small to medium `xml` data we can use DOM style parsing, but for large XML files we can use event driven parsing.

JSON

In the web or REST world the most predominant choice of data exchange format is **JavaScript Object Notation (JSON)**-let us familiarize ourselves with the advantages of using JSON. JSON is replacing XML as a de-facto standard format for data exchange, and many NOSQL databases accept or recognize JSON as first class citizens. JSON format is language independent and can be parsed with many existing programming languages, including R. We will learn the JSON syntax and how to access JSON data with R.

There are several packages that allow importing, exporting, and manipulating JSON data. Some of them are `rjson`, `RJSONIO`, and `jsonlite`. `rjson` is still used in some R-based API wrappers. The simplest way of reading JSON data is:

```
install.packages("jsonlite")
library(jsonlite)
install.packages('curl')
library(curl)
hadley_orgs <- fromJSON("https://api.github.com/users/hadley/orgs")
```

The previous code calls GitHub online code repository APIs to get live data on almost all activity – this gives R `dataframe` which can be manipulated easily. The output is as shown in the following screenshot:

If you want the raw JSON we can convert the data frame into JSON string using the following function:

```
json <- toJSON(hadley_orgs)
json
```

The output is as shown in the following screenshot:

```
> json
[{"login":"ggobi","id":423638,"url":"https://api.github.com/orgs/ggobi","repos_url":"https://api.github.com/orgs/ggobi/repos","events_u
rl":"https://api.github.com/orgs/ggobi/events","members_url":"https://api.github.com/orgs/ggobi/members{/member}","public_members_url":
"https://api.github.com/orgs/ggobi/public_members{/member}","avatar_url":"https://avatars.githubusercontent.com/u/423638?v=3"},{"login"
:"rstudio","id":513560,"url":"https://api.github.com/orgs/rstudio","repos_url":"https://api.github.com/orgs/rstudio/repos","events_url"
:"https://api.github.com/orgs/rstudio/events","members_url":"https://api.github.com/orgs/rstudio/members{/member}","public_members_url"
:"https://api.github.com/orgs/rstudio/public_members{/member}","avatar_url":"https://avatars.githubusercontent.com/u/513560?v=3"},{"log
in":"rstats","id":722735,"url":"https://api.github.com/orgs/rstats","repos_url":"https://api.github.com/orgs/rstats/repos","events_url"
:"https://api.github.com/orgs/rstats/events","members_url":"https://api.github.com/orgs/rstats/members{/member}","public_members_url":"
https://api.github.com/orgs/rstats/public_members{/member}","avatar_url":"https://avatars.githubusercontent.com/u/722735?v=3"},{"login"
:"ropensci","id":1200269,"url":"https://api.github.com/orgs/ropensci","repos_url":"https://api.github.com/orgs/ropensci/repos","events_
url":"https://api.github.com/orgs/ropensci/events","members_url":"https://api.github.com/orgs/ropensci/members{/member}","public_member
s_url":"https://api.github.com/orgs/ropensci/public_members{/member}","avatar_url":"https://avatars.githubusercontent.com/u/1200269?v=3
","description":""},{"login":"rjournal","id":3330561,"url":"https://api.github.com/orgs/rjournal","repos_url":"https://api.github.com/o
rgs/rjournal/repos","events_url":"https://api.github.com/orgs/rjournal/events","members_url":"https://api.github.com/orgs/rjournal/memb
ers{/member}","public_members_url":"https://api.github.com/orgs/rjournal/public_members{/member}","avatar_url":"https://avatars.githubu
sercontent.com/u/3330561?v=3"},{"login":"rstats-db","id":5695665,"url":"https://api.github.com/orgs/rstats-db","repos_url":"https://api
.github.com/orgs/rstats-db/repos","events_url":"https://api.github.com/orgs/rstats-db/events","members_url":"https://api.github.com/org
s/rstats-db/members{/member}","public_members_url":"https://api.github.com/orgs/rstats-db/public_members{/member}","avatar_url":"https:
//avatars.githubusercontent.com/u/5695665?v=3"}]
```

```
Json  <- fromJSON("D:/R/Chapter_2/catalogue.json")
```

The previous code reads a `Json` file and creates a R list. The output looks like this:

```
Json
```

```
> Json
$catalog
$catalog$book
   id      author                title    genre price
1 b1 Avinash Paul       Text Mining Computer   100
2 b2 Ashish Kumar Advance Text Mining Computer   200
```

If we want to put a `json` file to `data.frame` we can use the following code:

```
catalogue <- fromJSON("D:/R/Chapter_2/catalogue.json")
catalogue.df <- do.call("rbind", lapply(catalogue, data.frame,
stringsAsFactors = FALSE))
View(catalogue.df)
```

The output is as shown in the following screenshot:

	row.names	book.id	book.author	book.title	book.genre	book.price
1	catalog.1	b1	Avinash Paul	Text Mining	Computer	100
2	catalog.2	b2	Ashish Kumar	Advance Text Mining	Computer	200

HTTP

To retrieve data from the web, we have to communicate with servers and web services. The protocol of communication on the web is **Hypertext Transfer Protocol (HTTP)**. It is the most common protocol for communication between web clients. The software that we use to browse the internet is called a browser, which knows how to communicate with servers over HTTP. HTTP provides 8 methods for communication: GET, POST, PUT, DELETE, HEAD, TRACE, OPTION, and CONNECT. The type of request we construct to communicate with the servers varies based on the method we choose. If we want to mine data from the web using R, we should be able to communicate with servers over HTTP.

For this purpose we will use the RCurl package.

The getURL() function uses the RCurl facilities to send the HTTP request and receive the response. It collects the body of the response into a single string and returns it:

```
htmlPage <- getURL("http://www.w3schools.com/html/html_tables.asp")
```

After executing the previous command, the variable htmlPage contains the source of the HTML page for the index.html file. This function can be used for screen scraping, namely the action of using a computer program to copy data from websites. The response can be passed to functions like htmlTreeParse() or xmlTreeParse(), to get valuable information from the web page.

You can to submit HTML forms via HTTP getForm() and postForm(). These correspond to the two different ways of submitting a form GET and POST. For forms using the GET action, the name equal to value pairs are appended to the URI, separated by &. For forms using the POST action, the name-value pairs are encoded in the body of the request. The following command is programmatically sending a query to Google to search for the keyword **Rcurl**:

```
getForm("http://www.google.com/search", q ="RCurl", hl = "en", ie = "ISO-8859-1", oe = "ISO-8859-1", btnG = "Google+Search")
```

In the previous section we discussed about GET and POST, but RCurl offer functions to deal with other HTTP methods as well. We can change the methods in calls to getURL() by making use of the customrequest option as shown following:

```
url <-"http://mywebsite.com/deleteUser"
res <- getURL(url = url, customrequest ="DELETE", header = TRUE)
```

Similarly, we can provide other methods such as PUT, or HEAD.

For redirect requests we can enable followlocation option:

```
res <- getURL(url = url, customrequest ="DELETE", header = TRUE,
followlocation = TRUE)
```

If you want to set it for all your requests you can use the RCurlOptions to set various parameters.

```
options(RCurlOptions = list(verbose = TRUE, followlocation = TRUE,
timeout = 100, useragent = "myApp in R"))
```

When I try to interact with a URL via https and it need to verify certificates we can use following command:

```
x = getURLContent("https://www.google.com",cainfo = "/Users/duncan/
cacert.pem")
```

In order to skip verification:

```
x = getURLContent("https://www.google.com",ssl.verifypeer = FALSE)
```

RCurl is powerful package that helps to make requests and to receive and process the incoming response. It is a bit bulky since lot of configurations has to be done for various options. Fortunately, there is a package that offers a simpler interface the httr package.

httr package is builds upon RCurl by wrapping the functions. It is organized by HTTP verbs and it provides convenient functions to configure additional request components as shown following is the list of functions or options that is present in both the packages:

Operations	RCurl	httr
Specify GET request	getURL(), getURLContent(), getForm()	GET()
Specify POST request	postForm()	POST()
Specify HEAD request	httpHEAD()	HEAD()

Operations	RCurl	httr
Specify PUT request	`httpPUT()`	`PUT()`
Extract response	`content <-` `getURLContent()`	`content()`
Specify curl handle	`getCurlHandle(),` `curl`	`handle()`
Specify curl options	`.opts`	`config()`
Specify glocal curl options	`options(RCUrlOptions` `= list()), .opts`	`set_config()`
Execute code with curl options		`with_config()`
Add headers to request	`httpheaders`	`add_headers()`
Authenticate via one type of HTTP authentication	`userpwd`	`authenticate()`
Specify proxy connection	`proxy`	`use_proxy()`
Specify User-Agent header field	`useragent`	`user_agent()`
Specify cookies	`cookiefile`	`set_cookies()`
Display HTTP status code	`getCurlInfo(handle)` `$response.code`	`http_status()`
Display R error if request fails		`stop_for_` `status()`
Display R warning if request fails		`warn_for_` `status()`
Return TRUE if returned status code is exactly 200		`url_ok()`
Return TRUE if returned status code is in the 200s	`url.exists()`	`url_success()`
Set maximum request time	`timeout`	`timeout()`
Provide more information about client–server communication	`verbose`	`verbose()`
Parse URL into constituent components		`parse_url()`
Replace components in parsed URL		`modify_url()`
Build URL string from parsed URL		`build_url()`

Databases

R has several packages to connect to databases. We can use packages like RMySQL to connect to MySQL, ROracle to connect to Oracele, RPostgreSQL to connect to PostgreSQL and RSQLite to establish a native connection to a specific DBMS. All these packages extends the DBI package to provide a driver and the detailed.

The inner workings allow the generic functions to connect, disconnect, and submit and track queries. The DBI package in R provides a uniform, client side interface to different database management systems, such as MySQL, PostgreSQL, and Oracle the database-specific packages implement these functions in database-specific ways. The value of this approach is that there is a common set of functions that are expected to work the same way:

1. Install the DBI package this is a database interface between R environment and other relational data bases:

   ```
   install.packages("DBI")
   library(DBI)
   ```

2. For communicating with MySQL we need to install RMySQL package this package is a database interface and MySQL driver for R:

   ```
   install.packages("RMySQL")
   library(RMySQL)
   ```

3. Load a driver for a MySQL type:

   ```
   mySQLDriver = dbDriver("MySQL")
   ```

4. Make a connection to the database management server:

   ```
   con = dbConnect(mySQLDriver, user="root", password="root", dbname
   = "test", host = "localhost")
   ```

5. Before making the connection to the database we have to make sure the data base server is up and running, we can download the MySQL software from http://dev.mysql.com/downloads/mysql/.

    How to install the database is not in the scope of this book, you can find various blogs and videos that explain this.

   Make sure the data base is running with user root password root has a data base by name test if you have different configuration replace the appropriate parameters:

6. List all the tables:

```
bListTables(con)
```

7. We get the following output:

```
> dbListTables(con)
character(0)
> |
```

This means there are no tables in the database `test`:

8. Let's create a table in the database using the following SQL script, you can use any GUI or run-it on your MySQL prompt:

```
CREATE TABLE Persons

(

Name varchar(255)

);
```

9. Now lest list the tables:

```
dbListTables(con)
```

The output as follows:

```
> dbListTables(con)
[1] "persons"
>
```

10. Let's read the content from the `Persons` table:

```
dbReadTable(con, "Persons", row.names = "Name")
```

The output as follows:

```
> dbReadTable(con, "Persons", row.names = "Name")
data frame with 0 columns and 0 rows
> |
```

Let's insert some value into the table now and try to retrieve the data. You can use the following script to insert the values into the table:

1. Lets insert 3 rows by using the following script:

```
INSERT INTO Persons VALUES ("Avinash");
INSERT INTO Persons VALUES ("Paul");
INSERT INTO Persons VALUES ("Text Mining");
```

2. Now let's retrieve the data:

```
dbReadTable(con, "Persons", row.names = "Name")
```

The output is as follows, it says 3 rows retrieved:

```
Console ~/
> dbReadTable(con, "Persons", row.names = "Name")
data frame with 0 columns and 3 rows
```

3. The `dbReadTable` function returns a data frame; let's store it into a variable and print the content:

```
TableData <- dbReadTable(con, "Persons", row.names = "Name")
```

4. When we execute the following command in R-studio we get:

```
View(TableData)
```

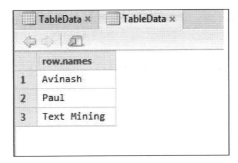

The `dbReadTable` function imports the Persons table from the database into R as a data frame, using the attribute `Name` as the row.names for the data frame. There are many other functions like `dbWriteTable`, `dbExistsTable`, and `dbRemoveTable`.

5. If we want to execute other queries like count, mean, or average, we can use the `dbGetQuery` function:

```
dbGetQuery(con,"SELECT COUNT(*) FROM Persons;")
```

6. If the results are huge, then getting all the results into R does not make sense, we can get it batch by batch by using dbSendQuery:

```
rs = dbSendQuery(con2, "SELECT * FROM Persons;")
firstBatch = fetch(rs, n = 500) ## get first 500 tuples
secondBatch = fetch(rs, n = 200) ## get next 200 tuples
dbHasCompleted(rs)
dbClearResult(rs)
```

7. When finished, we should free up resources by disconnecting and unloading the driver:

```
dbDisconnect(con)
dbUnloadDriver(mySQLDriver)
```

Another approach to work with DBMS via R is to use RODBC. This package uses open database connectivity ODBC drivers as way to connect to DBMS, and requires that the user installs and configures the necessary driver before using it in R. ODBC drivers are available across all platforms and for a wide variety of DBMS. They even exist for data storage formats that are not databases, like CSV, XLS or XLSX. The package also gives a general approach for managing different types of databases with the same set of functions. This approach depends on whether ODBC drivers are available for the DBMS type to be used in combination with the platform R is working on.

In order to use the following package, we have to first make sure we have the ODBC driver for the required RDBMS. In the example previous We connected to MySQL database so I will show you how to connect to the same database using ODBC.

We can use RODBC package to query RDBMS on ODBC Bridge. In order to use this we must download and install the right version of MySQL connector based on our operating system and bit version. You can download it from: https://dev.mysql. com/downloads/connector/odbc/

After downloading `mysql-connector-odbc-5.3.4-winx64.msi` for Windows, execute it and follow the instruction in the wizard. After successful installation, we need to configure the connection, as shown in the following screenshot:

1. Click on **Control Panel**:

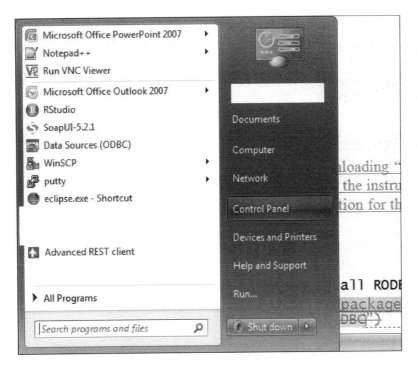

2. Select **Administrative Tools**:

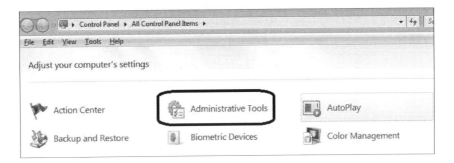

3. Select **Data Sources (ODBC)**:

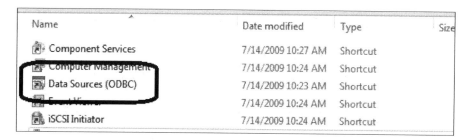

4. Select **System DNS** and click on **Add** button:

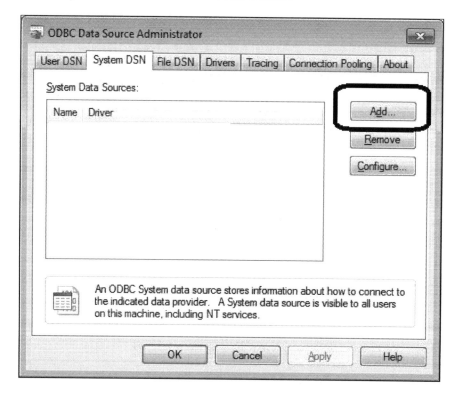

5. Select **MySQL ODBC 5.3 ANSI Driver** and click on **Finish**:

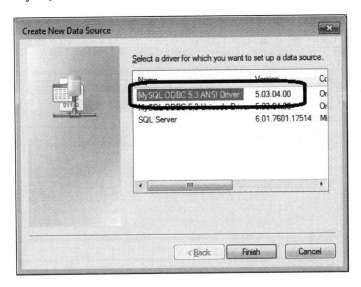

6. Configure the database details, then click on **Test Connection** once its successful, select the DB you want connect to:

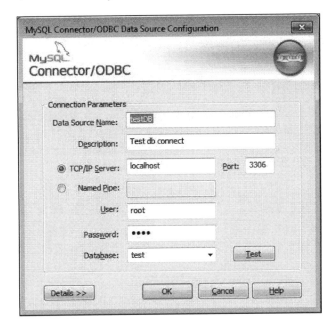

7. Once all the previous steps are successful, install RODBC:

```
install.packages("RODBC")
```

8. Load RODBC package:

```
library(RODBC)
```

9. Create a connection to the database:

```
testDB <- odbcConnect("testDB")
```

10. Get the list of tables:

```
Tables <- sqlTables(testDB)

View(Tables)
```

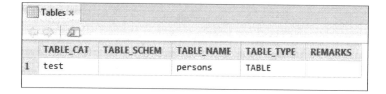

11. Query the database and put the results into the dataframe:

```
dataframe <- sqlQuery(testDB, " SELECT * FROM persons")
View(dataframe)
```

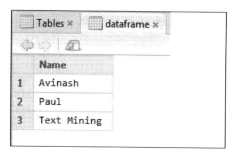

Processing text using regular expressions

The web consists predominantly of unstructured text. One of the main tasks in web scraping is to collect the relevant information from heaps of textual data. Within the unstructured text we are often interested in specific information, especially when we want to analyze the data using quantitative methods. Specific information can include numbers such as phone numbers, zip codes, latitude, longitude, or addresses.

First, we gather the unstructured text, next we determine the recurring patterns behind the information we are looking for, and then we apply these patterns to the unstructured text to extract the information. When we are web scraping, we have to identify and extract those parts of the document that contain the relevant information. Ideally, we can do so using xpath althrough, sometimes the crucial information is hidden within values. Sometimes relevant information might be scattered across an HTML document. We need to write regular expressions to retrieve data from such documents. Regular expressions provide us with syntax for systematically accessing patterns in text.

Let's see some basic string manipulation using `stringr` package:

- To extract a sub-string of a string, let's use `str_extract(string, pattern)`:

```
install.packages("stringr")
library(stringr)
simpleString <-"Lets learn about text. Ahh! learn text mining."
str_extract(simpleString , "learn")
[1] "learn" # returned the match

str_extract(simpleString , "learning")

[1] NA # could not find match
```

- Returns all the occurrences of the given string in list format:

```
str_extract_all(simpleString , "learn")
unlist(str_extract_all(simpleString , "learn"))

[1] "learn" "learn"
```

- Character matching is case sensitive. Thus, capital letters in regular expressions are different from lowercase letters:

```
str_extract(simpleString , "LEARN")

[1] NA # could not find match
```

- We can change this behavior by enclosing a string with `ignore.case()`:

```
str_extract(simpleString , ignore.case("LEARN"))
```

- A string is simply a sequence of characters. We can match characters or sequence of characters white space:

```
unlist(str_extract_all(simpleString , "rn"))
unlist(str_extract_all(simpleString , "Lets le"))
```

- When we need to find out if the string starts with and ends with specific characters, there are two simple additions we can make to our regular expression to specify locations. The caret symbol (^) at the beginning of a regular expression marks the beginning of a string, and $ at the end marks the end:

```
str_extract_all(c("apple","apricot","peach"),"^a")


[[1]]
[1] "a" # apple starts with 'a'


[[2]]
[1] "a" # apricot starts with 'a'


[[3]] # No 'a' in the begning
character(0)
```

- Pipe (|). This character is treated as an OR operator the function returns all matches to the expressions before and after the pipe:

```
str_extract_all(simpleString , "learn|text")
```

- In order to write more flexible, generalized search queries, we can use the following expressions. The period character matches any character:

```
str_extract(simpleString,"t.xt")
```

- A character class means that any of the characters within the brackets will be matched:

```
str_extract(simpleString,"t[ei]xt")
```

- The previous code extracts the word text, as the character e is part of the character class [ei]. We can add ranges of characters using a dash -.In this case, any characters from e to i are valid matches:

```
str_extract(simpleString,"t[e-i]xt")
```

The following table lists predefined character classes in R regular expressions:

`[:digit:]`	Digits: 0 1 2 3 4 5 6 7 8 9
`[:lower:]`	Lowercase characters: a–z
`[:upper:]`	Uppercase characters: A–Z
`[:alpha:]`	Alphabetic characters: a–z and A–Z
`[:alnum:]`	Digits and alphabetic characters
`[:punct:]`	Punctuation characters: ., ;, and so on.
`[:graph:]`	Graphical characters: `[:alnum:]` and `[:punct:]`
`[:blank:]`	Blank characters: Space and tab
`[:space:]`	Space characters: Space, tab, newline, and other space characters
`[:print:]`	Printable characters: `[:alnum:]`, `[:punct:]`, and `[:space:]`

In order to use the predefined classes, we have to enclose them in brackets. Otherwise, R assumes that we are specifying a character class consisting of the constituent characters. The following code matches all the words that begin with t and end with t:

```
str_extract(simpleString,"t[[:alpha:]][[:alpha:]]t")
```

A more readable way is:

```
str_extract(simpleString,"t[[:alpha:]]{2}t")
```

The following table lists the quantifiers in regular expressions:

?	The preceding item is optional and will be matched at most once
*	The preceding item will be matched zero or more times
+	The preceding item will be matched one or more times
{n}	The preceding item is matched exactly n times
{n, }	The preceding item is matched n or more times
{n,m}	The preceding item is matched at least n times, but not more than m times

These quantifiers are very powerful and comes handy when we construct regular expressions.

The following table lists symbols with special meaning:

\w	Word characters: `[[:alnum:]_]`
\W	No word characters: `[^[:alnum:]_]`
\s	Space characters: `[[:blank:]]`
\S	No space characters: `[^[:blank:]]`
\d	Digits: `[[:digit:]]`
\D	No digits: `[^[:digit:]]`
\b	Word edge
\B	No word edge
\<	Word beginning
\>	Word end

Now that we have understood some basics of regular expression, let's take the following messy text and extract name and numbers out of it:

```
"3456-2345tom hank(999) 555-0113 Geo, James555-6542Dr. Paul lee485
0945ted frank345-234-56879Steel, Peter5553642Mr. Bond"
```

The code would be as follows:

```
mixedString <-"3456-2345tom hank(999) 555-0113 Geo, James555-6542Dr.
Paul lee485 0945ted frank345-234-56879Steel, Peter5553642Mr. Bond"
name <- unlist(str_extract_all(mixedString,"[[:alpha:].,]{2,}"))
```

The output is as shown following:

```
> name <- unlist(str_extract_all(mixedString,"[[:alpha:].,]{2,}"))
> name
 [1] "tom"    "hank"   "Geo,"   "James"  "Dr."    "Paul"   "lee"    "ted"    "frank"  "Steel," "Peter"  "Mr."    "Bond"
```

- To extract the names, we used the regular expression `[[:alpha:].,]{2,}`:
  - We used the character class `[:alpha:]`, which tells us that we are looking for alphabetic characters
  - Names can also contain periods, commas and empty spaces, which we want to add to the character class to read `[[:alpha:].,]`
  - Add restriction that the contents of the character class have to be matched at least twice
  - We have to specify that we only want matches of at least length two

- To get numbers, we can use the following regex:

```
numbers <- unlist(str_extract_all(mixedString,"\\(?(\\d{3})?\\)?(-
|)?\\d{3}(-|)?\\d{4}"))
```

- If we want the location of a match in a given string, we use the functions: `str_locate()` or `str_locate_all()`:

```
str_locate(simpleString,"text")
```

- We can extract substring using:

```
str_sub(simpleString, start = 12, end = 1)
```

- For replacements we can use `str_replace()` and `str_replace_all()`:

```
str_replace(example.obj, pattern ="text", replacement ="data")
```

- To split a string into several smaller strings we can use:

```
str_split(simpleString,"[[:blank:]]")
```

- In order to detect a pattern in string we can use the `str_detect()` function:

```
str_detect(simpleString,"text")
```

- If we need to know the number of occurrences of a word we can use:

```
str_count(simpleString,"text")
```

- To add characters to the edges of strings or trim blank `spaces.str_pad()` and `str_trim()` we can use:

```
str_trim(simpleString)
```

- We can join strings using the `str_c()` function:

```
words <- c("lets","learn","text","mining")
sentence <- str_c(words, collapse =" ")
```

- One way to deal with messy text data is the `agrep()` function, which provides approximate matching via the Levenshtein distance. Function `agrep()` matches substrings of each element of the string that is searched for, just like `grep()`, and not the entire word itself:

```
agrep("Rahul Dravid","Rahul k Dravid", max.distance = list(all =
3))
```

- We can change the maximum distance between pattern and string by adjusting both the `max.distance` and the costs parameter. The higher the `max.distance` parameter, the more approximate matches it will find. Using the costs parameter you can adjust the costs for the different operations necessary to liken to strings.

- While dealing with text encoding plays a significant role, using the function `iconv()`, we can translate a string from one encoding scheme to another:

```
text.utf8 <- iconv("text", from ="windows-1252", to ="UTF-8")
```

- Explore tau package form R It has lot of useful methods related to encoding and translation.

Tokenization and segmentation

In this topic, we will learn techniques that can be applied for the tokenization and segmentation of text, to analyze and get some useful information about the text.

Word tokenization

Tokenization is the process of breaking up a stream of text, a character sequence or a defined document unit, into phrases, words, symbols, or other meaningful elements called tokens. The goal of tokenization is the exploration of the words in a sentence. Before we do any kind on analysis on the text using a language processor, we need to normalize the words. When we do quantitative analysis on the text we consider it a bag of words. and extract the key words, frequency of occurrence, and the importance of each word in the text. Tokenizing provides various kind of information about text, like the number of words or tokens in a text, the vocabulary or the type of words.

Some terminologies we need to know are listed as follows:

- **Sentence**: Unit of written language
- **Utterance**: Unit of spoken language
- **Word form**: The inflected form as it actually appears in the corpus
- **Lemma**: An abstract form, shared by word forms having the same stem and part of speech
- **Word sense**: Stands for the class of words with stem
- **Types**: Number of distinct words in a corpus (vocabulary size)
- **Tokens**: Total number of words

Use the following code to find all the data sets available in:

```
data(package = .packages(all.available = TRUE))
```

If you need to check the data sets available in a specific package, you may specify the package name as the argument.

Let's import a data set available in `tm` package and build a document term matrix:

```
library(tm)
data(acq)
```

Create a document term matrix:

```
tdm <- TermDocumentMatrix(acq)
```

Access document IDs, terms and their number of a term document matrix:

```
Docs(tdm)
nDocs(tdm)
nTerms(tdm)
Terms(tdm)
```

Operations on a document-term matrix

We will now see how various operations on document term matrix work:

- **Frequent terms**: From the document-term matrix created in previous section, let's try to find out the number of terms occurring more than or equal to 30 times.

  ```
  findFreqTerms(tdm,30)
  ```

  ```
   [1] "and"      "company" "dlrs"    "for"     "from"    "has"
  "its"      "mln"
   [9] "pct"      "reuter"  "said"    "shares"  "stock"   "that"
  "the"      "was"
  [17] "will"     "with"    "would"
  ```

- **Term association**: Correlation is a quantitative measure of the co-occurrence of words in multiple documents, so we need to provide a term document matrix as the input to the function and a correlation limit; for example if we provide cottelation limit as 0.70 that function will return terms that have a search term co-occurrence of at least 70% and more.

Let's find out the words that correlate to word `stock` with the correlation of atleast 0.70:

```
findAssocs(tdm, "stock", 0.70)
```

```
       stock
believe     0.80
several     0.80
would       0.75
all         0.71
business.   0.71
partial     0.71
very        0.71
```

Let us see a couple of tokenizers from different packages in R:

- The generated term document matrix may be huge. The size of our DTM is 50 X 2013 It says 96% of the rows are zero, that is, the majority of words will appear in a few documents. We can reduce the sparsity of the document for computational `efficiency.inspect(tdm)`:

  ```
  <<TermDocumentMatrix (terms: 2103, documents: 50)>>
  Non-/sparse entries: 4135/101015
  Sparsity: 96%
  Maximal term length: 21
  Weighting: term frequency (tf)
  ```

- The output shows that 96% of the terms occur just a few times, thus the document term matrix becomes large even for a small sized data set. We need to remove the sparse terms:

  ```
  inspect(removeSparseTerms(tdm, 0.3))
  ```

  ```
  <<TermDocumentMatrix (terms: 5, documents: 50)>>
  Non-/sparse entries: 231/19
  Sparsity         : 8%
  Maximal term length: 6
  Weighting          : term frequency (tf)
  ```

- Sparsity is reduced from 96% to 8%:

```
library(tm)


# convert to lower case
acq <- tm_map(acq, content_transformer(tolower))


#remove whitespaces
acq <- tm_map(acq, stripWhitespace)


#remove stop words(english)
acq <- tm_map(acq, removeWords, stopwords("english"))


s <- "i am learning text mining. This is exciting . lot to explore
Mr. Paul."



MC_tokenizer(s)
```

```
 [1] "i"         "am"         "learning" "text"       "mining"     ""
"This"      "is"         "exciting"
[10] ""           ""           "lot"       "to"         "explore" "Mr"
""           "Paul"       ""
```

- This tokenizer is producing 18 tokens, we can see it has removes periods and considered it as a empty token:

```
scan_tokenizer(s)



 [1] "i"         "am"         "learning" "text"       "mining." "This"
"is"         "exciting" "."
[10] "lot"       "to"         "explore" "Mr."       "Paul"       "!"
```

- This tokenizer is producing 15 tokens

- `RWeka` package provides word, n-gram and alphabetic tokenizers:
  ```
  install.packages("RWeka")library(RWeka)
  ```

  ```
  WordTokenizer(s, control = NULL)
  ```

  ```
   [1] "i"        "am"       "learning" "text"      "mining"   "This"
  "is"       "exciting" "lot"
   [10] "to"       "explore"  "Mr"       "Paul"
  ```

- When we run the previous tokenizer we get 13 tokens with all the punctuation cleaned:
  ```
  NGramTokenizer(s, control = NULL)
  ```

  ```
   [1] "i am learning"      "am learning text"     "learning text
  mining"
   [4] "text mining This"   "mining This is"       "This is
  exciting"
   [7] "is exciting lot"    "exciting lot to"      "lot to
  explore"
   [10] "to explore Mr"     "explore Mr Paul"      "i am"
   [13] "am learning"       "learning text"        "text mining"
   [16] "mining This"       "This is"              "is exciting"
   [19] "exciting lot"      "lot to"               "to explore"
   [22] "explore Mr"        "Mr Paul"              "i"
   [25] "am"                "learning"             "text"
   [28] "mining"            "This"                 "is"
   [31] "exciting"          "lot"                  "to"
   [34] "explore"           "Mr"                   "Paul"
  ```

  ```
  AlphabeticTokenizer(s, control = NULL)
  ```

  ```
   [1] "i"        "am"       "learning" "text"      "mining"   "This"
  "is"
   [8] "exciting" "lot"      "to"        "explore"  "Mr"        "Paul"
  ```

`kRp.POS.tags` is a function in koRpus package, which can be used get a set of POS tags for a given language. It supports English(en), German(de), Spanish(es), French(fr), Italian(it), and Russian(ru).

- Install TreeTagger and set the environment to tell the `tree-tagger` function in koRpus where is it installed:

```
install.packages("koRpus")library(koRpus)

set.kRp.env(TT.cmd="~/bin/treetagger/cmd/tree-tagger", lang="en")

get.kRp.env(TT.cmd=TRUE)
```

We can extract the vocabulary of this sentence by filtering out repeating words, abbreviation and counting words which has same lemma as one. We can build out own tokenizer.

There are various challenges to tokenization some of them are listed as following:

- **New York**: Should we keep it as one token or Two?
- **TEXT**: should we convert all the tokens to lower case?
- **MS, PhD**: how to handle abbreviations.
- **Ernst and Young**: Should we consider this as one word?
- **Bangalore's weather**: how to handle apostrophes' should we convert it to Bangalore, Bangalores
- **I'm, isn't**: Should we choose to expand them to "I am", "is not"

Sentence segmentation

Sentence segmentation is the process of determining the longest unit of words. This task involves determining sentence boundaries, and we know most languages have punctuation to define the end of sentence. Sentence segmentation is also referred as sentence boundary disambiguation, sentence boundary detection. Some of the factors that effects Sentence segmentation is language, character set, algorithm, application, data source. Sentences in most of the languages are delimited by punctuation marks, but the rules for punctuation can vary dramatically. Sentences and sub sentences are punctuated differently in different languages. So for successful sentence segmentation understanding uses of punctuation in that language is important.

Let's consider english as the language, recognizing boundaries must be fairly simple since it has a rich punctuation system like periods, question marks, exclamation. But a period can become quite ambiguous since period can also be used for abbreviations like Mr., representing decimal numbers like 1.2, or abbreviations.

Let's look at R openNLP packages and function `Maxent_Sent_Token_Annotator`.

Generate an annotator which computes sentence annotations using the apache OpenNLP maxent sentence detector:

```
install.packages(openNLP)

library(openNLP)

s <- "I am learning text mining. This is exciting.lot to explore Mr.
Paul!"


sentence.boundaries <- annotate(s,Maxent_Sent_Token_Annotator(language =
"en", probs = FALSE, model = NULL))


sentences <- s[sentence.boundaries]
```

The output of detected sentences is as shown following:

```
id type      start end features
 1 sentence      1  26
 2 sentence     28  45
 3 sentence     47  71
```

Normalizing texts

Normalization in text basically refers to standardization or canonicalization of tokens, which we derived from documents in the previous step. The simplest scenario possible could be the case where query tokens are an exact match to the list of tokens in document, however there can be cases when that is not true. The intent of normalization is to have the query and index terms in the same form. For instance, if you query U.K., you might also be expecting U.K.

Token normalization can be performed either by implicitly creating equivalence classes or by maintaining the relations between unnormalized tokens. There might be cases where we find superficial differences in character sequences of tokens, in such cases query and index term matching becomes difficult. Consider the words anti-disciplinary and anti-disciplinary. If both these words get mapped into one term named after one of the members of the set for example anti-disciplinary, text retrieval would become so efficient. Query on one of the terms would fetch the documents containing either of the terms. We will deal with the asymmetric query expansion in detail in upcoming chapters.

Lemmatization and stemming

Grammar in every language allows usage of derivationally related words with similar meaning, which are nothing but different forms of the same word. Such as develop, developing, developed. The intent of performing lemmatization and stemming revolves around a similar objective of reducing inflectional forms and map derived words to the common base form.

Stemming is a process of chopping off the ends of words, mostly derivational affixes. Lemmatization is a more efficient process, which uses vocabulary and morphological analysis of words and removes only the inflectional endings to return the base form of word as output.

Stemming

RWeka provides stemming functions to remove the common derivational affixes:

```
> IteratedLovinsStemmer("cars", control = NULL)

[1] "car"


> LovinsStemmer("ponies", control = NULL)

[1] "pon"
```

Lemmatization

The wordnet package can be utilized to effectively perform lemmatization. The WordNet database needs to be downloaded and installed, and the installed path needs to be specified before R wordnet package can be used.

After downloading WordNet, set the WNHOME environment variable to use the path where WordNet installation can be found:

```
Sys.setenv(WNHOME = "~/WordNet-3.0")


initDict("~/WordNet-3.0/dict/")


setDict("~/WordNet-3.0/dict")


getIndexTerms(pos, maxLimit, filter)


where, pos is the part of speech type, can be either "NOUN","VERB","ADJEC
TIVE","ADVERB"
```

```
>getFilterTypes()
```

```
[1] "ContainsFilter"     "EndsWithFilter"     "ExactMatchFilter"
"RegexFilter"
[5] "SoundFilter"        "StartsWithFilter" "WildcardFilter"
```

You can use either of the filter types to fetch the index terms:

```
>if(initDict()) {
       filter <- getTermFilter("StartsWithFilter", "beer", TRUE)
       getIndexTerms("NOUN", 3, filter)
   }
```

```
[[1]]
[1] "Java-Object{Lemma: beer  POS: noun  Tag-Sense-Count: 1\nList of
Synsets (1)\n  #1: 7886849\nList of Pointers (3)\n  #1: @ (Hypernym)\n
#2: ~ (Hyponym)\n  #3: + (Derivationally related form)}"
```

```
[[2]]
[1] "Java-Object{Lemma: beer barrel  POS: noun  Tag-Sense-Count: 0\nList
of Synsets (1)\n  #1: 2823335\nList of Pointers (1)\n  #1: @ (Hypernym)}"
```

```
[[3]]
[1] "Java-Object{Lemma: beer bottle  POS: noun  Tag-Sense-Count: 1\nList
of Synsets (1)\n  #1: 2823428\nList of Pointers (1)\n  #1: @ (Hypernym)}"
```

```
> if(initDict()) {
       filter <- getTermFilter("EndsWithFilter", "beer", TRUE)
       getIndexTerms("NOUN", 3, filter)
   }
```

```
[[1]]
[1] "Java-Object{Lemma: beer  POS: noun  Tag-Sense-Count: 1\nList of
Synsets (1)\n  #1: 7886849\nList of Pointers (3)\n  #1: @ (Hypernym)\n
#2: ~ (Hyponym)\n  #3: + (Derivationally related form)}"
```

```
[[2]]
```

[1] "Java-Object{Lemma: birch beer POS: noun Tag-Sense-Count: 0\nList of Synsets (1)\n #1: 7927716\nList of Pointers (1)\n #1: @ (Hypernym)}"

[[3]]

[1] "Java-Object{Lemma: bock beer POS: noun Tag-Sense-Count: 0\nList of Synsets (1)\n #1: 7887461\nList of Pointers (1)\n #1: @ (Hypernym)}"

Synonyms

Let's refer the following example:

```
>if(initDict()) {
    filter <- getTermFilter("EndsWithFilter", "organisation", TRUE)
    getIndexTerms("NOUN", 3, filter)
 }
```

[[1]]
[1] "Java-Object{Lemma: business organization POS: noun Tag-Sense-Count: 0\nList of Synsets (1)\n #1: 8061042\nList of Pointers (5)\n #1: @ (Hypernym)\n #2: ~ (Hyponym)\n #3: %m (Member meronym)\n #4: ; ([Unknown])\n #5: - ([Unknown])}"

[[2]]
[1] "Java-Object{Lemma: disorganization POS: noun Tag-Sense-Count: 0\nList of Synsets (2)\n #1: 14500341\n #2: 552922\nList of Pointers (2)\n #1: @ (Hypernym)\n #2: + (Derivationally related form)}"

[[3]]
[1] "Java-Object{Lemma: european law enforcement organisation POS: noun Tag-Sense-Count: 0\nList of Synsets (1)\n #1: 8210042\nList of Pointers (1)\n #1: @ (Hypernym)}"

Alternaively,
>synonyms("organisation","NOUN")

```
 [1] "administration"  "arrangement"   "brass"          "constitution"
 [5] "establishment"   "formation"     "governance"     "governing
body"
 [9] "organisation"    "organization"  "system"
```

Lexical diversity

Consider a speaker, who uses the term allow multiple times throughout the speech, compared to an another speaker who uses terms allow, concur, acquiesce, accede, and avow for the same word. The latter speech has more lexical diversity than the former. Lexical diversity is widely believed to be an important parameter to rate a document in terms of textual richness and effectiveness.

Lexical diversity, in simple terms, is a measurement of the breadth and variety of vocabulary used in a document. The different measures of lexical diversity are TTR, MSTTR, MATTR, C, R, CTTR, U, S, K, Maas, HD-D, MTLD, and MTLD-MA.

koRpus package in R provides functions to estimate the lexical diversity or complexity.

If N is the total number of tokens and V is the number of types:

Measure	Description	Wrapper Function (koRpus package in R)
TTR	Type-Token Ratio	TTR
MSTTR	Mean segment type token ratio	MSTTR
C	logTTR	C.ld
R	Root TTR	R.ld
CTTR	Corrected TTR	CTTR
U	Uber Index	U.ld
S	Summer index	S.ld

Analyse lexical diversity

This function provides all the lexical diversity measure characteristics as described previously. If you are only interested in estimating one of the measures, then you can use the wrapper functions as mentioned in table instead of lex.div:

```
Library(koRpus)
Lex.div(tagged.txt))

ttr.res <- TTR(tagged.text, char=TRUE)
```

Calculate lexical diversity

This function is truncated version of lex.div, as argument it just requires the number of token and types and calculates the lexical diversity. Lexical diversity measures like TTR, C, R, CTTR, U, S, and Maas can be estimated by using this function:

```
lex.div.num(N, V)
```

Readability

Readability provides quantitative measures to analyze the complexity and quality of a text document.

Automated readability index

AIR is a readability test to gauge the understandability of a text document:

$$AIR = \frac{No\ of\ letter,\ punctuation\ marks\ and\ numbers ¿}{Number\ of\ spaces} ¿ + 0.5 \frac{Number\ of\ spaces ¿}{Number\ of\ sentences} ¿ AIR =$$

$$\frac{No\ of\ letter,\ punctuation\ marks\ and\ numbers ¿}{Number\ of\ spaces} ¿ + 0.5 \frac{Number\ of\ spaces ¿}{Number\ of\ sentences} ¿ - 21.43$$

- 21.43

```
Library(koRpus)
AIR(tagged.text))
```

The function does not count the syllables, when the parameter is specified as "NRI", navy Readability index is calculated while if it set to "simple", simplified formula is calculated.

Apart from ARI, koRpus package provides different functions for readability analysis like bormuth, **Degree** of **Reading Power(DRP)**, **Easy Listening Formula(ELF)**, dickes.steiwer, danielson.bryan, dale.chall to estimate different readability indices.

Language detection

TextCat is a text classification utility. The primary usage of TextCat is language identification. `textcat` package in R provides wrapper function for n-gram based text categorization and the language detection. It can detect up to 75 languages:

```
Library(textcat)
>my.profiles <- TC_byte_profiles[names(TC_byte_profiles)]
>my.profiles


A textcat profile db of length 75.


> my.text <- c("This book is in English language",
 "Das ist ein deutscher Satz.",
 "Il s'agit d'une phrase française.",
 "Esta es una frase en espa~nol.")
 textcat(my.text, p = my.profiles)
> textcat(my.text, p = my.profiles)


[1] "english" "german"  "french"  "spanish"
```

Summary

After accessing the data, processing it in different ways and having inspected it using multiple measures, we now have the cleansed data for advanced analysis. In the upcoming chapter, you will learn about advanced text processing techniques and text categorization.

3

Categorizing and Tagging Text

In corpus linguistics, text categorization or tagging into various word classes or lexical categories is considered to be the second step in NLP pipeline after tokenization. We have all studied parts of speech in our elementary classes; we were familiarized with nouns, pronouns, verbs, adjectives, and their utility in English grammar. These word classes are not just the salient pillars of grammar, but also quite pivotal in many language processing activities. The process of categorizing and labeling words into different parts of speeches is known as *parts of speech tagging* or simply *tagging*.

The goal of this chapter is to equip you with the tools and the associated knowledge about different tagging, chunking, and entailment approaches and their usage in natural language processing.

Earlier chapters focused on basic text processing; this chapter improvises on those concepts to explain the different approaches of tagging texts into lexical categories, chunking methods, statistical analysis on corpus data, and textual entailment.

In this chapter, we will cover the following topics:

- Parts of speech tagging
- Hidden Markov Models for POS tagging
- Collocation and contingency tables
- Feature extraction
- Log-linear models
- Textual entailment

Parts of speech tagging

In text mining we tend to view free text as a bag of tokens (words, n-grams). In order to do various quantitative analyses, searching and information retrieval, this approach is quite useful. However, when we take a bag of tokens approach, we tend to lose lots of information contained in the free text, such as sentence structure, word order, and context. These are some of the attributes of natural language processing which humans use to interpret the meaning of given text. NLP is a field focused on understanding free text. It attempts to understand a document completely like a human reader.

POS tagging is a prerequisite and one of the most import steps in text analysis. POS tagging is the annotation of the words with the right POS tags, based on the context in which they appear, POS taggers categorize words based on what they mean in a sentence or in the order they appear. POS taggers provide information about the semantic meaning of the word. POS taggers use some basic categories to tag different words — some basic tags are noun, verb, adjective, number and proper noun. POS tagging is also important for information extraction and sentiment analysis.

POS tagging with R packages

Let us see how to tag a text with R OpenNLP package.

The parts of speech Tagger tags each token with their corresponding parts of speech, utilizing lexical statistics, context, meaning, and their relative position with respect to adjacent tokens. The same token may be labeled with multiple syntactic labels based on the context. Or some word tokens may be labeled with X POS tag (in Universal POS Tagger) to denote short-hand for common words or misspelled words. POS tagging helps a great deal in resolving lexical ambiguity. R has an OpenNLP package that provides POS tagger functions, leveraging maximum entropy model:

```
library("NLP")
library("openNLP")
library("openNLPdata")
```

Let's take a simple and short text as shown in the following code:

```
s <- "Pierre Vinken , 61 years old , will join the board as a
nonexecutive director Nov. 29 .Mr. Vinken is chairman of Elsevier N.V.
, the Dutch publishing group ."
str <- as.String(s)
```

First, we will annotate the sentence using the function `Maxent_Sent_Token_` `Annotator ()`; we can use different models for different languages. The default language used by the functions is en `language="en"`, which will use the default model under the language en that is under `OpenNLPdata`, that is, `en-sent.bin`:

```
sentAnnotator <- Maxent_Sent_Token_Annotator(language = "en", probs =
TRUE, model =NULL)
```

The value for the model is a character string giving the path to the `Maxent` model file to be used, `NULL` indicating the use of a default model file for the given language.

You can explore the available mode files at:

```
http://opennlp.sourceforge.net/models-1.5/
```

```
annotated_sentence <- annotate(s,sentAnnotator)
annotated_sentence
```

The output of the preceding code is as shown in the following screenshot. Let's look at how to interpret the output:

```
> annotated_sentence
 id type     start end features
  1 sentence     1  90 prob=0.530237
  2 sentence    92 157 prob=0.9952137
```

- The **id** column is just a numbering of the number of detected sentences
- The **start** column denotes the character at which the sentence started
- The **end** column denotes the character at which the sentence ended
- The **features** columns tells us the confidence level or the probability of the detected sentences

In order to apply the `id` to actual text, that is to find out all the sentences, we can pass the actual text to the annotator object as shown in the following code:

```
actualSentence <- str
actualSentence [annotated_sentence]
```

```
> actualSentence [annotated_sentence]
[1] "Pierre Vinken , 61 years old , will join the board as a nonexecutive director Nov. 29 .Mr."
[2] "Vinken is chairman of Elsevier N.V. , the Dutch publishing group ."
>
```

Once we have annotated the sentence we can go to the next step of annotating the words. We can annotate each word by passing the annotated sentence to a word annotator `Maxent_Word_Token_Annotator ()` as shown in the following code. We can use different models for different languages. The default language is en. This uses the model that is under `OpenNLPdata`, that is, `en-token.bin`:

```
wordAnnotator <- Maxent_Word_Token_Annotator(language = "en", probs =
TRUE, model =NULL)
annotated_word<-  annotate(s,wordAnnotator,annotated_sentence)
```

We have to pass the sentence to the word annotator function. If the sentence annotator is not executed — that is if the sentences are not annotated — the word annotator will produce an error as shown in the following screenshot:

```
Error in e(s, a) : no sentence token annotations found
> |
```

```
annotated_word
head(annotated_word)
```

Let's look at the output shown here and understand how to interpret it:

- The **id** column is just a numbering of the number of detected sentences/words
- The **start** column denotes the character at which the word started
- The **end** column denotes the character at which the word ended
- The **features** columns tells us the confidence level or the probability of the detected words

```
> annotated_word
 id type      start end features
  1 sentence      1  90 prob=0.530237, constituents=<<integer,18>>
  2 sentence     92 157 prob=0.9952137, constituents=<<integer,12>>
  3 word          1   6 prob=1
  4 word          8  13 prob=1
  5 word         15  15 prob=1
  6 word         17  18 prob=1
  7 word         20  24 prob=1
  8 word         26  28 prob=1
  9 word         30  30 prob=1
 10 word         32  35 prob=1
 11 word         37  40 prob=1
 12 word         42  44 prob=1
 13 word         46  50 prob=1
 14 word         52  53 prob=1
 15 word         55  55 prob=1
 16 word         57  68 prob=1
 17 word         70  77 prob=1
 18 word         79  82 prob=0.9909137
 19 word         84  85 prob=1
 20 word         87  90 prob=0.7791815
 21 word         92  97 prob=1
 22 word         99 100 prob=1
 23 word        102 109 prob=1
 24 word        111 112 prob=1
 25 word        114 121 prob=1
 26 word        123 126 prob=0.7611589
 27 word        128 128 prob=1
 28 word        130 132 prob=1
 29 word        134 138 prob=1
 30 word        140 149 prob=1
 31 word        151 155 prob=1
 32 word        157 157 prob=1
```

Now, we are going to do POS tagging on the sentence to which we have applied both sentence and word annotator.

We can use different models for different languages. The default is en; it uses the model that is under OpenNLPdata, that is, en-pos-maxent.bin.

If needed, we can load a different model as shown in the following code:

```
install.packages("openNLPmodels.en", repos = "http://datacube.wu.ac.
at/", type = "source")
library("openNLPmodels.en")
pos_token_annotator_model <- Maxent_POS_Tag_Annotator(language = "en",
probs = TRUE, model = system.file("models", "en-pos-perceptron.bin",
package = "openNLPmodels.en"))
```

For this example, we will go ahead with the default model. First, the POS model must be loaded into the memory from disk or other source:

```
pos_tag_annotator <- Maxent_POS_Tag_Annotator(language = "en", probs = TRUE, model =NULL)
pos_tag_annotator
```

```
> pos_tag_annotator
An annotator inheriting from classes
  Simple_POS_Tag_Annotator Annotator
with description
  Computes POS tag annotations using the Apache OpenNLP Maxent Part of Speech tagger employing the default model for language 'en'
>
```

The POS tagger instance is now ready to tag data. It expects a tokenized sentence as input, which is represented as a string array; each string object in the array is one token:

```
posTaggedSentence <- annotate(s, pos_tag_annotator, annotated_word)
posTaggedSentence
head(posTaggedSentence)
```

From the following screenshot, we can see that each word contains one parts of speech tag, the start and the end index of the word, and the confidence scores of each tag:

```
> posTaggedSentence
 id type      start end features
  1 sentence     1  90 prob=0.530237, constituents=<<integer,18>>
  2 sentence    92 157 prob=0.9952137, constituents=<<integer,12>>
  3 word         1   6 prob=1, POS=NNP, POS_prob=0.9476405
  4 word         8  13 prob=1, POS=NNP, POS_prob=0.9692841
  5 word        15  15 prob=1, POS=,, POS_prob=0.9884445
  6 word        17  18 prob=1, POS=CD, POS_prob=0.9926943
  7 word        20  24 prob=1, POS=NNS, POS_prob=0.9893489
  8 word        26  28 prob=1, POS=JJ, POS_prob=0.9693832
  9 word        30  30 prob=1, POS=,, POS_prob=0.9873552
 10 word        32  35 prob=1, POS=MD, POS_prob=0.9460105
 11 word        37  40 prob=1, POS=VB, POS_prob=0.9865564
 12 word        42  44 prob=1, POS=DT, POS_prob=0.9692801
 13 word        46  50 prob=1, POS=NN, POS_prob=0.9928681
 14 word        52  53 prob=1, POS=IN, POS_prob=0.9592474
 15 word        55  55 prob=1, POS=DT, POS_prob=0.9890297
 16 word        57  68 prob=1, POS=JJ, POS_prob=0.7213763
 17 word        70  77 prob=1, POS=NN, POS_prob=0.987327
 18 word        79  82 prob=0.9909137, POS=NNP, POS_prob=0.9263844
```

Let's concentrate on the distribution of POS tags for word tokens:

```
posTaggedWords <- subset(posTaggedSentence, type == "word")
```

Extract only the features from the annotator:

```
tags <- sapply(posTaggedWords$features, `[[`, "POS")
tags
```

```
> tags
 [1] "NNP" "NNP" ","   "CD"  "NNS" "JJ"  ","   "MD"  "VB"  "DT"  "NN"
"NNP" "NNP" ","   "IN"  "DT"  "JJ"  "NN"  "NNP" "CD"  "."   "NNP" "VBZ" "NN"  "IN"
[26] "DT"  "JJ"  "NN"  "NN"  "."
```

table(tags), in the following screenshot, we can see the number of tags present in the sentence, for example, how many "noun, proper, singular", "noun, common, plural" are present, and many more:

```
> table(tags)
tags
  ,   .  CD  DT  IN  JJ  MD  NN NNP NNS  VB VBZ
  3   2   2   3   2   3   1   5   6   1   1   1
>
```

Let's extract word/POS pairs to make it more readable:

```
sprintf("%s -- %s", str[posTaggedWords], tags)
```

This prints all the words and their tags side by side for easy reading, as shown in the following screenshot:

```
> sprintf("%s -- %s", str[posTaggedWords], tags)
 [1] "Pierre -- NNP"     "Vinken -- NNP"        ", -- ,"
", -- ,"
        [8] "will -- MD"        "join -- VB"          "the -- DT"
"nonexecutive -- JJ"
        [15] "director -- NN"    "Nov. -- NNP"         "29 -- CD"
"chairman -- NN"
        [22] "of -- IN"          "Elsevier -- NNP"     "N.V. -- NNP"
"publishing -- NN"
        [29] "group -- NN"       ". -- ."

"61 -- CD"              "years -- NNS"        "old -- JJ"

"board -- NN"           "as -- IN"            "a -- DT"

".Mr. -- ."             "Vinken -- NNP"       "is -- VBZ"

", -- ,"                "the -- DT"           "Dutch -- JJ"
```

The tag set used by the English POS model is the Penn Treebank tag set. The following is a list of tags and their description:

Table reference http://www.comp.leeds.ac.uk/amalgam/tagsets/upenn.html.

Some of the common tag sets are as follows:

Number	Tag	Description
1	CC	Coordinating conjunction
2	CD	Cardinal number
3	DT	Determiner
4	EX	Existential there
5	FW	Foreign word
6	IN	Preposition or subordinating conjunction
7	JJ	Adjective
12	NN	Noun, singular or mass
13	NNS	Noun, plural
14	NNP	Proper noun, singular
15	NNPS	Proper noun, plural
16	PDT	Predeterminer
17	POS	Possessive ending
18	PRP	Personal pronoun
19	PRP$	Possessive pronoun
25	TOTo	
26	UH	Interjection
27	VB	Verb, base form
28	VBD	Verb, past tense
33	WDT	Wh-determiner
34	WP	Wh-pronoun

We can use a tag dictionary, which specifies the tags each token can have. Using a tag dictionary has two advantages. Firstly, inappropriate tags can not bee assigned to tokens in the dictionary, and secondly, the beam search algorithm has to consider fewer possibilities and can search faster. Various pre-trained POS models for OpenNLP can be found at:

```
http://opennlp.sourceforge.net/models-1.5/
```

Hidden Markov Models for POS tagging

Hidden Markov Models (HMM) are conducive to solving classification problems with generative sequences. In natural language processing, HMM can be used for a variety of tasks such as phrase chunking, parts of speech tagging, and information extraction from documents. If we consider words as input, while any prior information on the input can be considered as states, and estimated conditional probabilities can be considered as the output, then POS tagging can be categorized as a typical sequence classification problem that can be solved using HMM.

Basic definitions and notations

According to (Rabiner), there are five elements needed to define an HMM:

- N denotes the number of states (which are hidden) in the model. For parts of speech tagging, N is the number of tags that can be used by the system. Each possible tag for the system corresponds to one state of the HMM. The possible interconnections of individual states are denoted by $S = \{S1, Sn\}$. Let qt denote the state at time t.

- Let M denote the number of distinct output symbols in the alphabet of the HMM. For parts of speech tagging, M is the number of words in the lexicon of the system. Let $V = \{v1 .. vm\}$ denote the set of observation symbols.

- The state transition probability distribution is also called the transition matrix $A = \{aij\}$, representing the probability of going from state Si to Sj. For parts of speech tagging, the states represent the tags, so aij is the probability that the model will move from tag ti to tj. This probability can be estimated using data from a training corpus:

$$a_{ij} = P\left[q_{t+1} = S_j \mid q_t = S_i\right] 1 \leq i, j \leq N$$

Where qt denotes the current state, the transition probabilities should also satisfy the normal stochastic constraints:

$$a_{ij} > 0, 1 \leq i, j \leq N$$

And:

$$\sum_{j=1}^{N} a_{ij} = 1, 1 \leq i, j \leq N$$

- An observation symbol probability distribution is also called emission matrix $B = \{bj(k)\}$, indicating the probability of the emission of symbol Vk when the system state is Sj:

$$b_j(k) = P\{o_t = v_k \mid q_t = s_j\}, 1 \le j \le N, 1 \le k \le M$$

Where $v_k v_k v_k v_k$ denotes the kth observation symbol and $o_t o_t o_t o_t$ the current parameter vector, the following conditions must be satisfied:

$$b_j(k) \ge 0, \le j \le N, 1 \le k \le M$$

And:

$$\sum_{k=1}^{M} b_j(k) = 1, 1 \le j \le N$$

- The initial state probability distribution $\pi = \{\pi_i\} \pi = \{\pi_i\}$ represents probabilities of initial states. For parts of speech tagging, this is the probability that the sentence will begin:

$$\pi_i = P[q_1 = S_i] 1 \le i \le N, \pi_i \ge 0 \sum_{k=1}^{N} \pi_i = 1$$

For an ngram model, if we need to estimate the probability of a word tag in a word sequence, we can estimate the conditional probability, given the information about the previous words in the sequence:

$$\left[\quad P(w1....wn) = Pe\,(w1).Pe(w2 \mid w1).Pe(w3 \mid w1 , w2) .... Pe(wn \mid wn\text{-}2 , wn \quad \right]$$

Implementing HMMs

When implementing an HMM, floating-point underflow is a significant problem. When we apply the Viterbi or forward algorithms to long sequences, the resultant probability values are very small, which can underflow on most machines. We solve this problem differently for each algorithm, as shown in the following examples.

Viterbi underflow

As the Viterbi algorithm only multiplies probabilities, a simple solution to underflow is to log all the probability values and then add values instead of multiplying. In fact, if all the values in the model matrices (A, B, π) are logged, then at runtime only addition operations are needed.

Forward algorithm underflow

The forward algorithm sums probability values, so it is not a viable solution to log the values in order to avoid underflow. The most common solution to this problem is to use scaling coefficients that keep the probability values in the dynamic range of the machine, and that are dependent only on t. The coefficient $c_i c_i c_i c_i$ is defined as:

$$c_t = \frac{\alpha_{t(i)}}{\sum_{i=1}^{n} \alpha_{t(i)}}$$

And thus the new-scaled value for a becomes:

$$\hat{\alpha}_{t(t)} = c_t * \alpha_{t(t)} = \frac{\alpha_{t(i)}}{\sum_{i=1}^{n} \alpha_{t(i)}}$$

OpenNLP chunking

The process of chunking consists of dividing a text into syntactically correlated parts of words, like noun groups, and verb groups, but does not specify their internal structure, or their role in the main sentence. We can use `Maxent_Chunk_Annotator()` for the `OpenNLP` R package to accomplish this.

Before we can use this method, we have to POS tag the sentence. We can use the same steps performed previously for POS tagging:

```
chunkAnnotator <- Maxent_Chunk_Annotator(language = "en", probs =
FALSE, model = NULL)
annotate(s,chunkAnnotator,posTaggedSentence)
head(annotate(s,chunkAnnotator,posTaggedSentence))
```

The `chunk` tag provides some more useful information:

```
▷ annotate(s,chunkAnnotator,posTaggedSentence)
id type     start end features
 1 sentence    1  90 prob=0.530237, constituents=<<integer,18>>
 2 sentence   92 157 prob=0.9952137, constituents=<<integer,12>>
 3 word         1   6 prob=1, POS=NNP, POS_prob=0.9476405, chunk_tag=B-NP
 4 word         8  13 prob=1, POS=NNP, POS_prob=0.9692841, chunk_tag=I-NP
 5 word        15  15 prob=1, POS=,, POS_prob=0.9884445, chunk_tag=O
 6 word        17  18 prob=1, POS=CD, POS_prob=0.9926943, chunk_tag=B-NP
 7 word        20  24 prob=1, POS=NNS, POS_prob=0.9893489, chunk_tag=I-NP
 8 word        26  28 prob=1, POS=JJ, POS_prob=0.9693832, chunk_tag=B-ADJP
 9 word        30  30 prob=1, POS=,, POS_prob=0.9873552, chunk_tag=O
10 word        32  35 prob=1, POS=MD, POS_prob=0.9460105, chunk_tag=B-VP
11 word        37  40 prob=1, POS=VB, POS_prob=0.9865564, chunk_tag=I-VP
12 word        42  44 prob=1, POS=DT, POS_prob=0.9692801, chunk_tag=B-NP
13 word        46  50 prob=1, POS=NN, POS_prob=0.9928681, chunk_tag=I-NP
14 word        52  53 prob=1, POS=IN, POS_prob=0.9592474, chunk_tag=B-PP
15 word        55  55 prob=1, POS=DT, POS_prob=0.9890297, chunk_tag=B-NP
16 word        57  68 prob=1, POS=JJ, POS_prob=0.7213763, chunk_tag=I-NP
17 word        70  77 prob=1, POS=NN, POS_prob=0.987327, chunk_tag=I-NP
18 word        79  82 prob=0.9909137, POS=NNP, POS_prob=0.9263844, chunk_tag=B-NP
```

Chunk tags

The chunk tags contain the name of the chunk type, for example, I-NP for noun phrase words and I-VP for verb phrase words. Most chunk types have two types of chunk tags: B-CHUNK for the first word of the chunk and I-CHUNK for each other word in the chunk. A chunk tag like B-NP is made up of two parts:

1. First part:

   ○ **B**: Marks the beginning of a chunk

   ○ **I**: Marks the continuation of a chunk

   ○ **E**: Marks the end of a chunk

A chunk may be only one word long or may contain multiple words (like *Pierre Vinken* in the preceding example).The O chunk tag is used for tokens which are not part of any chunk.

1. Second part:

   ○ **NP**: Noun chunk

   ○ **VP**: Verb chunk

You can find chunks for different languages at:

`http://opennlp.sourceforge.net/models-1.5/`

Collocation and contingency tables

When we look into a corpus, some words tend to appear in combination; for example, *I need a strong coffee, John kicked the bucket, He is a heavy smoker*. J. R. Firth drew attention to such words that are not combined randomly into a phrase or sentence. Firth coined the term collocations for such word combinations; the meaning of a word is in part determined by its characteristic collocations. In the field of **natural language processing (NLP)**, the combination of words plays an important role.

Word combinations that are considered collocations can be compound nouns, idiomatic expressions, or combinations that are lexically restricted. This variability in definition is defined by terms such as **multi-word expressions (MWE)**, **multi-word units (MWU)**, bigrams and idioms.

Collocations can be observed in corpora and can be quantified. Multi-word expressions have to be stored as units in order to understand their complete meaning. Three characteristic properties emerge as a common theme in the linguistic treatment of collocations: semantic non-compositionality, syntactic non-modifiability, and the non-substitutability of components by semantically similar words (Manning and Schutze 1999, 184). Collocations are words that show mutual expectancy, in other words, a tendency to occur near each other. Collocations can also be understood as statistically salient patterns that can be exploited by language learners.

Extracting co-occurrences

There are basically three types of co-occurrences found in lexical data. The attraction or statistical association in words that co-occur is quantified by co-occurrence frequency.

Surface Co-occurrence

While extracting co-occurrences using this methodology, the criteria is that the surface distance is measured in word tokens. Let's consider the following sentence:

The wind blew heavily the umbrella went rolling.

2L   1L node 1R   2R

In the preceding span, umbrella is the node word, L stands for left, R's stand for right and numbers stand for distance. The words in the collocation that span around the node word can be symmetric (*L2, R2*) or asymmetric (*L2, R1*). This is the traditional approach in corpus linguistics and lexicography.

For example, let's consider a simple sentence: *A great degree of judgment is required to catch a cricket ball. A player must practice day in day out to gain agility and improve fielding techniques. When the batsman strokes, the ball rolls at a high speed. Sometimes the fielder has to dive or slide to stop the rolling ball. If the fielder is lazy, it rolls and rolls to the boundary.*

Let's consider two words:

w1 = ball

w2 = roll

Let the span window be symmetric with two words (*L2, R2*), limited by sentence boundaries.

We can see the co-occurrence frequency $f = 2$ and the number of times the words occur independently, that is, marginal frequency $f1 = 3, f2 = 4$.

$f1, f2$ is called the marginal frequency, that is, how many times the words *w1* and *w2* occurred independently in the highlighted spans.

Textual co-occurrence

While extracting co-occurrences using this methodology, some of the criteria we take into account are that words co-occur if they are in the same segment, for example in the same sentence, paragraph, or document.

Syntactic co-occurrence

In this type of co-occurrence, words have a specific syntactic relation. Usually, they are word combinations of a chosen syntactic pattern, like *adjective + noun*, or *verb + preposition*, depending on the preferred multi-word expression structural type. In order to do this, corpus is lemmatized, POS-tagged and parsed, since these steps are independent of any language. Word *w1* and *w2* are said to co-occur only if there is a syntactic relation between them. This type of co-occurrence can help to cluster nouns that are used as objects of the same verb, such as tea, water, and cola, which are all used with the verb drink. Consider the following example:

Open	Bar
Mixed	Crowd
Young	Men
Drinking	Cola
Young	Ladies
Drinking	Wine
Drinking	Tea

It was a open invitation, to a party with an open bar. There was a mixed crowd. Young men were in the center drinking cola, young ladies to the right drinking wine. The old gentlemen were drinking tea.

If we calculate the co-occurrence frequency of young men, it's $f = 1$ the number of times the words occur independently, for example, marginal frequency is $f1 = 2, f2 = 1$.

Co-occurrence frequency is a quantitative measure of affinity between words based on their recurrence. This frequency is not sufficient, because lot or bigrams such as *is to* and *and the* occur in a corpus very frequently.

Co-occurrence in a document

If two words *w1* and *w2* are seen in the same document, they are usually related by topic. In this form of co-occurrence, how near or far away from each other the words are in the document or the order of their appearance is irrelevant. Document-wise co-occurrence has been successfully used in NLP.

Co-occurrence in a single document may talk about multiple topics, so we can investigate the word co-occurrence in a smaller segment of text such as a sentence. In contrast to the document-wise model, sentence-wise co-occurrence does not consider the whole document, and only considers the number of times those two words occur in the same sentence.

We consider each textual unit as a sentence; multiple occurrences of a word in the same sentences are ignored. Let's consider the same text as mentioned previously:

- A great degree of judgment is required to catch a cricket ball
- A player must practice day in day out to gain agility and improve fielding techniques
- When the batsman strokes, the ball rolls at a high speed
- Sometimes the fielder has to dive or slide to stop the rolling ball
- If the fielder is lazy, it rolls and rolls to the boundary

We can see the Co-occurrence frequency $f = 2$ and the number of times the words occur independently, for example, marginal frequency $f1 = 3, f2 = 3$.

Quantifying the relation between words

In corpus linguistics, the statistical association or attraction between words is expressed in the form of a contingency table. Significance testing is applied to estimate the degree of association or difference between two words. An independence model is hypothesized between the words and is tested for a good fit. The worse the fit, the more associated the words are.

Contingency tables

Contingency tables are basically used to demonstrate the relationship between categorical variables. We can even call it a categorical equivalent of scatterplots.

For measuring association in contingency tables, we can apply a statistical hypothesis test with null hypothesis H0: independence of rows and columns. H0 implies there is no association between w1 and w2 and the association score is equal to the test statistic or p-value, as shown in the following diagram:

2. Compare observed frequencies O_{ij} to expected frequencies E_{ij} under H0 (→ later) I or estimate conditional prob. $Pr(w2 \mid w1)$, $Pr(w1 \mid w2)$, ands so on, maximum-likelihood estimates or confidence intervals. Following is a simple contingency table for word *w1* and *w2*:

	* | w2	* | -w2	
w1 |*	O11	O12	= f1
-w1 |*	O21	O22	

   = f2   =N

	* | cola	* | -cola	
drinking |*	1	2	=3
-drinking |*	1	4	

   =2   =8

Chi-square and fisher-test functions in the base package can be used to estimate the association scores. Contingency tables in R are represented in matrix format:

 Use functions like `Chisq.test(M)` for chi-squared independence test and `fisher.test(M)` for fisher test on a contingency table stored as M.

Let's apply this on bigrams in brown corpus. Data can be downloaded from (Please provide the link to the dataset `brown_bigrams.tbl.txt`).

```
rown <- read.table("brown_bigrams.tbl.txt",header=TRUE)
Names(rown)
#The output as below
[1] "id"     "word1" "pos1"  "word2" "pos2"  "O11"   "O12"   "O21"
"O22"
# we are going to make the observed frqeuncies as numeric
cols<-c(6:9)
Brown[,cols] = apply(Brown[,cols], 2, function(x) as.numeric(x))
# Lets calculate the rowsum A1,A2, colsum B1,B2 and the sample size Z
Brown <- transform(Brown, A1=O11+O12, A2=O21+O22, B1=O11+O21,
B2=O12+O22, Z=O11+O12+O21+O22)
# The expected frquencies can be estimated as
Brown <- transform(Brown, E11=(A1*B1)/Z, E12=(A1*B2)/Z, E21=(A2*B1)/Z,
E22=(A2*B2)/Z)
# Significance Measures :
# Chi-squared statistics
Brown$chisq = Z * (abs(O11*O22 - O12*O21) - Z/2)^2 / (A1 * A2 * B1 *
B2)
Brown$log<- 2*( ifelse(O11>0, O11*log(O11/E11), 0) + ifelse(O12>0,
O12*log(O12/E12), 0) + ifelse(O21>0, O21*log(O21/E21), 0) +
ifelse(O22>0, O22*log(O22/E22), 0))
```

Detailed analysis on textual collocations

```
text <- "Customer value proposition has become one of the most widely
used terms in business markets in recent years. Yet our management-
practice research reveals that there is no agreement as to what
constitutes a customer value proposition—or what makes one persuasive.
Moreover, we find that most value propositions make claims of savings
and benefits to the customer without backing them up. An offering
may actually provide superior value—but if the supplier doesn't
demonstrate and document that claim, a customer manager will likely
dismiss it as marketing puffery. Customer managers, increasingly
held accountable for reducing costs, don't have the luxury of simply
believing suppliers' assertions.
```

Customer managers, increasingly held accountable for reducing costs, don't have the luxury of simply believing suppliers' assertions. Take the case of a company that makes integrated circuits (ICs). It hoped to supply 5 million units to an electronic device manufacturer for its next-generation product. In the course of negotiations, the supplier's salesperson learned that he was competing against a company whose price was 10 cents lower per unit. The customer asked each salesperson why his company's offering was superior. This salesperson based his value proposition on the service that he, personally, would provide. Unbeknownst to the salesperson, the customer had built a customer value model, which found that the company's offering, though 10 cents higher in price per IC, was actually worth 15.9 cents more. The electronics engineer who was leading the development project had recommended that the purchasing manager buy those ICs, even at the higher price. The service was, indeed, worth something in the model—but just 0.2 cents! Unfortunately, the salesperson had overlooked the two elements of his company's IC offering that were most valuable to the customer, evidently unaware how much they were worth to that customer and, objectively, how superior they made his company's offering to that of the competitor. Not surprisingly, when push came to shove, perhaps suspecting that his service was not worth the difference in price, the salesperson offered a 10-cent price concession to win the business—consequently leaving at least a half million dollars on the table. Some managers view the customer value proposition as a form of spin their marketing departments develop for advertising and promotional copy. This shortsighted view neglects the very real contribution of value propositions to superior business performance. Properly constructed, they force companies to rigorously focus on what their offerings are really worth to their customers. Once companies become disciplined about understanding customers, they can make smarter choices about where to allocate scarce company resources in developing new offerings."

```
library(tm)
library(SnowballC)
text.corpus <- Corpus(VectorSource(text))
```

Few standard text preprocessing:

```
text.corpus <- tm_map(text.corpus, stripWhitespace)
text.corpus <- tm_map(text.corpus, tolower)
text.corpus <- tm_map(text.corpus, removePunctuation)
text.corpus <- tm_map(text.corpus, removeWords, stopwords("english"))
text.corpus <- tm_map(text.corpus, stemDocument)
text.corpus <- tm_map(text.corpus, removeNumbers)
```

Tokenizer for n-grams and passed on to the term-document matrix constructor:

```
library(RWeka)
length <- 2 # how many words either side of word of interest
length1 <- 1 + length * 2
ngramTokenizer <- function(x) NGramTokenizer(x, Weka_control(min =
length, max = length1 ))
text.corpus <- tm_map(text.corpus, PlainTextDocument)
dtm <- TermDocumentMatrix(text.corpus, control = list(tokenize =
ngramTokenizer))
inspect(dtm)
```

When we inspect the `TermDocumentMatrix`, the output is as shown in the following data:

```
<<TermDocumentMatrix (terms: 188, documents: 1)>>
Non-/sparse entries: 188/0
Sparsity           : 0%
Maximal term length: 98
Weighting          : term frequency (tf)


Terms
character(0)
  ability communicate mindset makes easy successful conversations
clients understand                     1
  absence opportunity form emotional bond technology falls short
frontline                              1
  advisers consider guardians customers wellbeing therefore full
confidence sell                        1
  advisers may mindset makes reluctant helpa hesitancy stem several
1
  advisers positive feelings values individual needsin short emotional
intelligencerequired                   1
  approaches complex protocols example may smooth simple customer
interactions                           1
```

Explore the term document matrix for all `ngrams` that have the node word `value` in them:

```
word <- 'value'
part_ngrams <- dtm$dimnames$Terms[grep(word, dtm$dimnames$Terms)]
part_ngrams
```

The following data shows the output:

```
[1] "advisers positive feelings values individual needsin short
emotional intelligencerequired"
[2] "behavior thoughts feelings values beliefs personal emotional
needs met"
[3] "belief products services offer values beliefs fear rejection
stemming"
[4] "elements largely govern human behavior thoughts feelings values
beliefs"
[5] "feelings lack belief products services offer values beliefs
fear"
[6] "feelings values beliefs personal emotional needs met unmet
consider"
[7] "feelings values individual needsin short emotional
intelligencerequired connect help"
[8] "govern human behavior thoughts feelings values beliefs personal
emotional"
[9] "human behavior thoughts feelings values beliefs personal
emotional needs"
[10] "lack belief products services offer values beliefs fear
rejection"
```

Keep only the ngrams of interest, as the following data shows:

```
part_ngrams <- part_ngrams[sapply(part_ngrams, function(i) {
  tmp <- unlist(strsplit(i, split=" "))
  tmp <- tmp[length(tmp) - length]
  tmp} == word)]
```

Find the collocated word in the ngrams:

```
col_word <- "customer"
part_ngrams <- part_ngrams[grep(col_word, part_ngrams)]
```

Count the collocations:

```
length(part_ngrams)
part_ngrams
```

Find collocations on both sides of the collocation of interest within the span specified:

```
alwords <- paste(part_ngrams, collapse = " ")
uniques <- unique(unlist(strsplit(alwords, split=" ")))
```

Left hand side collocations:

```
LHS <- data.frame(matrix(nrow = length(uniques), ncol = length(part_
ngrams)))
for(i in 1:length(part_ngrams)){
```

Estimate the position of unique words along the `ngram` vector:

```
position1 <- sapply(uniques, function(x) which(x ==
unlist(strsplit(part_ngrams[[i]], split=" "))))
```

Position of word of interest along `ngram`:

```
position2 <- which(word == unlist(strsplit(part_ngrams[[i]], split="
")) )
```

Estimate distance of all collocations to the word of interest:

```
dist <- lapply(position1, function(i) position2 - i )
```

Keeps only positive values:

```
dist <- lapply(dist, function(i)  i[i>0][1]   )
tmp <- rep(NA, length(uniques))
tmp <- tmp[1:length(unlist(unname(dist)))] <- unlist(unname(dist))
LHS[,i] <- tmp
}
row.names(LHS) <- uniques
```

Estimate the mean distance between the two words:

```
LHS_means <- rowMeans(LHS, na.rm = TRUE)
countN <- function ( v ) sum( !is.na( v ) )
LHS_freqs <- apply(LHS, 1, countN )
LHS_means <- data.frame(word = names(LHS_means),
                        mean_dist = unname(LHS_means),
                        freq = unname(LHS_freqs))
```

Sort by average distance:

```
LHS_means <- LHS_means[with(LHS_means, order(mean_dist)), ]
```

Sort based on frequency:

```
LHS_means <- LHS_means[with(LHS_means, order(-freq)), ]
Right hand side colocs:
RHS <- data.frame(matrix(nrow = length(uniques), ncol = length(part_
ngrams)))
for(i in 1:length(part_ngrams)){
```

Find the position of unique words along the `ngram` vector:

```
pos1 <- sapply(uniques, function(x) which(x == unlist(strsplit(part_
ngrams[[i]], split=" "))))
```

Find the position of the word of interest alongthe `ngram` vector:

```
pos2 <- which(word == unlist(strsplit(part_ngrams[[i]], split=" "))
)
```

Compute the distance of all `colocs` to word of interest:

```
dist <- lapply(pos1, function(i) pos2 - i )
```

Keep only positive values:

```
dist <- lapply(dist, function(i)  i[i<0][1]  )
```

Insert distance values into a vector to append into a data frame :

```
tmp <- rep(NA, length(uniques))
  tmp <- tmp[1:length(unlist(unname(dist)))] <- unlist(unname(dist))
  RHS[,i] <- tmp
}
row.names(RHS) <- uniques
```

Compute the mean distance between the two words:

```
RHS_means <- rowMeans(RHS, na.rm = TRUE)
```

Also get `coloc` frequencies in spans:

```
Function to count non-NA values: countN <- function ( v ) sum( !is.na(
v ) )
RHS_freqs <- apply(RHS, 1, countN )
RHS_means <- data.frame(word = names(RHS_means),
                    mean_dist = unname(RHS_means),
                    freq = unname(RHS_freqs))
Sort by mean distance:
RHS_means <- RHS_means[with(RHS_means, order(-mean_dist)), ]
```

Sort by frequency:

```
RHS_means <- RHS_means[with(RHS_means, order(-freq)), ]
```

Compute mutual information for all words in the span.

Mutual information is a measure of collocational strength. A collocation is a sequence of words or terms that co-occur more often. The higher the mutual information, the stronger the relation between the words:

```
MI <- vector(length = length(uniques))
for(i in 1:length(uniques)){
```

A = frequency of node word:

```
A <- length(grep(word, unlist(strsplit(exampl, split=" "))))
```

B = frequency of collocation:

```
B <- length(grep(uniques[i], unlist(strsplit(exampl, split=" "))))
```

Size of corpus = number of words in total:

```
sizeCorpus <- length(unlist(strsplit(exampl, split=" ")))
```

Span = span of words analysed to L and R of node word:

```
span <- span
```

Compute MI:

```
MI[i] <- log ( (A * B * sizeCorpus) / (A * B * span) ) / log (2)
```

Feature extraction

Feature extraction is a very important and valuable step in text mining. A system that can extract features from text has potential to be used in lots of applications. The initial step for feature extraction would be tagging the document; this tagged document is then processed to extract the required entities that are meaningful.

The elements that can be extracted from the text are:

- **Entities**: These are some of the pieces of meaningful information that can be found in the document, for example, location, companies, people, and so on
- **Attributes**: These are the features of the extracted entities, for example the title of the person, type of organization, and so on
- **Events**: These are the activities in which the entities participate, for example, dates

Textual Entailment Human communication is diverse in terms of the usage of different expressions to communicate the same message. This proves to be quite a challenging problem in natural language processing. Consider, for example, s and s'. If the meaning of s can be inferred from the meaning of s', it can be concluded that s entails s'. s can be termed as 'text', while s' is its 'hypothesis'; usually s' is the short statement, whereas s is a longer span of text. Textual entailment is directional in nature, which implies if s entails s', it does not mean s' necessarily entails s.

Textual entailment aims to infer the sense of form in a given text. From a language perspective it can consist of several types, for example, syntactic entailment, *I am going home* entails *I am going*, semantic entailment, *He is not happy* entails *He is unhappy*, and implicative entailment, *He fell down the stair* entails *He is injured*.

Entailment is the key capability for enhancing the performance in a wide variety of NLP tasks, such as question-answering systems, information retrieval, enhanced search engines, multi-document summarization, and machine translation.

There are various approaches of estimating textual entailment:

- Semantic similarity based methods
- The syntactic similarity based approach
- The logic based method
- The vector space model approach
- The surface string similarity based approach
- Machine learning based methods

Among the various approaches of textual entailment, semantic similarity is the most common. This method utilizes the similarity between concepts/senses to conclude whether the hypothesis can truly be inferred from the text. Similarity measures can quantify how alike the two concepts are. An auto can be considered more like a car than a house, since auto and car share vehicle as a common ancestor with an is-a hierarchy.

Lexical databases like WordNet are extremely effective for similarity measures, since they maps nouns and verbs into hierarchies of an is-a relationship.

Synonymy and similarity

The lexical unit S entails S' if they are synonyms as per WordNet, or if there is any association of similarity between them. For example, rise and lift, reveal and discover, grant and allow.

Let the entailment rule be designed as:

```
entails(S, S') IF synonymy(S, S') OR WN_similarity(S, S')
synonymy(rise,lift)= TRUE => entails(rise,lift)= TRUE
WN_similarity(reveal,dicover)= TRUE => entails(reveal,discover) = TRUE
```

First, download WordNet data and set WNHOME. Specify the Dict folder with the setDict command.

Install WordNet by downloading the .exe from:

```
http://wordnetcode.princeton.edu/2.1/WordNet-2.1.exe.
```

Library(WordNet) for Windows operating system uses the following command:

```
setDict("C:/Program Files (x86)/WordNet/2.1/dict")
Find_synonyms<- function(x){
filter <- getTermFilter("ExactMatchFilter", x, TRUE)
terms <- getIndexTerms("NOUN", 1, filter)
synsets <- getSynonyms(terms[[1]])
}
```

Multiwords, negation, and antonymy

WordNet contains many multi-words which have useful semantic relations with other words, but it may require additional processing to normalize them in order to use them effectively. There can be variation due to lemmatization, acronym dot or different spellings. In order to accurately measure the similarity, fuzzy matching is implemented using levenshtein distance between the WordNet words and the candidate word. Matching is allowed if the two compared words differ by less than 10%.

In the dependency tree, if there is any negation relation between the leaves and the father, the negation is spread across the tree until the root node. The entailment is not possible in this case:

```
Find_antonyms <- function(x){
    filter <- getTermFilter("ExactMatchFilter", x, TRUE)
    terms <- getIndexTerms("ADJECTIVE", 5, filter)
    synsets <- getSynsets(terms[[1]])
    related <- tryCatch(
        getRelatedSynsets(synsets[[1]], "!"),
        error = function(condition) {
            message("No direct antonym found")
            if(condition$message == "RcallMethod: invalid object
parameter")
                message("there is no exact antonym")
```

```
        else
            stop(condition)
        return(NULL)
    }
  )
  if (is.null(related))
      return(NULL)
  return(sapply(related, getWord))
}
Hypernomy and WordNet entailment
```

Concept similarity

In concept similarity we measure the similarity between two concepts, for example, if we consider *car* as one concept then it is more related to the concept *vehicle* than some other concept such as *food*. Similarity is measured by information contained in a *is-a* hierarchy. WordNet is a lexical database that is well suited for this purpose, since nouns and verbs are organized in an *is-a* hierarchy.

Path length

The elementary idea of estimating similarity based on the path length is that the similarity between concepts can be expressed as a function of path length between concepts and concept position. There are different variants of path length calculation to quantify the concept similarity as a function of path length:

- **Shortest Path length**: The shorter the path between the words/senses in a hierarchy graph, the more similar the words are:

  Path length between two words S = number of edges in shortest path

- Shortest path length with depth:

$$Similarity_{path}(c_1, c_2) = 2 * deep\_max - len(c_1, c_2)$$

- **C1 , C2** are the concepts.
- **len(C1,C2)** is the shortest path function between two concepts C1, C2.
- **deep_max** is a fixed value for the specific version of WordNet.

This measure expresses the similarity between two words in terms of a linear combination of the shortest path and depth of the sub-tree, which holds very useful information about the features of the words. The lower the sub-tree is in the hierarchy, the lesser the abstract meaning shared by the two words:

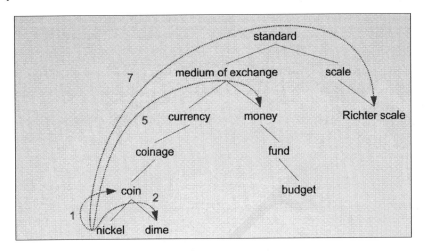

Resnik similarity

Resnik similarity estimates the similarity between relatedness of words in terms of information content. The proportion of the amount of information content shared by two concepts determines the semantic similarity between them. Resnik considers the position of the nouns in the *is-a* hierarchy. Let C be the concepts in taxonomy, allowing several inheritances. The key to finding similarity between concepts lies in the edge count of the hierarchy graph and the proportion of the information shared between the concepts with respect to a highly specific concept, which is higher in the hierarchy and consumes both of them.

If P(concept) is the probability of encountering a concept, and entity A belongs to the *is-a* hierarchy under B, then *P(A)<= P(B)*:

$$Similarity_{resnik}(c_1,c_2) = -\log p\big(lso(c_1,c_2)\big) = 2IC\big(lso(c_1,c_2)\big)$$

- **C1**, **C2** are the concepts
- **IC(C1)** Information content based measure of concept C1
- **IC(C2)** Information content based measure of concept C2

- **lso(C1,C2)** is the lowest common subsume of C1 C2

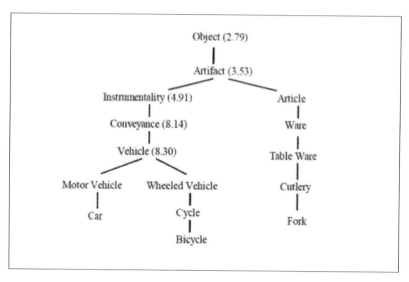

Lin similarity

Lin similarity estimates the semantic association between two-concepts/senses in terms of the ratio of the amount of information shared between two concepts to the total amount of information stored in the two concepts. It uses both the information required to describe the association between concepts and the information required to completely describe both of them:

$$Similarity_{Lin}(c_1, c_2) = \frac{2 * IC(lso(c_1, c_2))}{IC(c_1) + IC(c_2)}$$

- **C1, C2** are the concepts
- **IC(C1)** Information content based measure of concept C1
- **IC(C2)** Information content based measure of concept C2
- **lso(C1,C2)** is the lowest common subsume of C1 C2

Jiang – Conrath distance

To calculate the distance between two concepts, Jiang-Conrath distance considers the information content of the concepts, along with the information content of the most specific subsumer:

$$distance_{jiang}\left(c_1,c_2\right)=\left(IC\left(c_1\right)+IC\left(c_2\right)\right)-2IC\left(lso\left(c_1,c_2\right)\right)$$

- **C1, C2** are the concepts
- **IC(C1)** Information content based measure of concept C1
- **IC(C2)** Information content based measure of concept C2
- **lso(C1,C2)** is the lowest common subsume of C1 C2

As this is a distance measure, the higher the score the less the similarity.

Summary

In this chapter, we learned the different text categorizing and tagging methods, and how words can be grouped into different lexical categories or parts of speech to analyze the syntactical structure of a sentence. We also learned the approaches that can be leveraged to build language models which can extract concepts or sense out of a sentence, using sentence entailment.

In subsequent chapters, we are going to learn more about practical approaches in performing real-time text mining tasks.

4
Dimensionality Reduction

Data volume and high dimensions pose an astounding challenge in text-mining tasks. Inherent noise and the computational cost of processing huge amount of datasets make it even more arduous. The science of dimensionality reduction lies in the art of losing out on only a commensurately small numbers of information and still being able to reduce the high dimension space into a manageable proportion.

For classification and clustering techniques to be applied to text data, for different natural language processing activities, we need to reduce the dimensions and noise in the data so that each document can be represented using fewer dimensions, thus significantly reducing the noise that can hinder the performance.

In this chapter, we will learn different dimensionality reduction techniques and their implementations in R:

- The curse of dimensionality
- Dimensionality reduction
- Correspondence analysis
- Singular vector decomposition
- ISOMAP – moving toward non-linearity

The curse of dimensionality

Topic modeling and document clustering are common text mining activities, but the text data can be very high-dimensional, which can cause a phenomenon called the *curse of dimensionality*. Some literature also calls it the *concentration of measure*:

- Distance is attributed to all the dimensions and assumes each of them to have the same effect on the distance. The higher the dimensions, the more similar things appear to each other.

- The similarity measures do not take into account the association of attributes, which may result in inaccurate distance estimation.

- The number of samples required per attribute increases exponentially with the increase in dimensions.

- A lot of dimensions might be highly correlated with each other, thus causing multi-collinearity.

- Extra dimensions cause a rapid volume increase that can result in high sparsity, which is a major issue in any method that requires statistical significance. Also, it causes huge variance in estimates, near duplicates, and poor predictors.

Distance concentration and computational infeasibility

Distance concentration is a phenomenon associated with high-dimensional space wherein pairwise distances or dissimilarity between points appear indistinguishable. All the vectors in high dimensions appear to be orthogonal to each other. The distances between each data point to its neighbors, farthest or nearest, become equal. This totally jeopardizes the utility of methods that use distance based measures.

Let's consider that the number of samples is n and the number of dimensions is d. If d is very large, the number of samples may prove to be insufficient to accurately estimate the parameters. For the datasets with number of dimensions d, the number of parameters in the covariance matrix will be d^2. In an ideal scenario, n should be much larger than d^2, to avoid overfitting.

In general, there is an optimal number of dimensions to use for a given fixed number of samples. While it may feel like a good idea to engineer more features, if we are not able to solve a problem with less number of features. But the computational cost and model complexity increases with the rise in number of dimensions. for instance, if n number of samples look to be dense enough for a one-dimensional feature space. For a k-dimensional feature space, n^k samples would be required.

Dimensionality reduction

Complex and noisy characteristics of textual data with high dimensions can be handled by dimensionality reduction techniques. These techniques reduce the dimension of the textual data while still preserving its underlying statistics. Though the dimensions are reduced, it is important to preserve the inter-document relationships. The idea is to have minimum number of dimensions, which can preserve the intrinsic dimensionality of the data.

A textual collection is mostly represented in the form of a term document matrix wherein we have the importance of each term in a document. The dimensionality of such a collection increases with the number of unique terms. If we were to suggest the simplest possible dimensionality reduction method, that would be to specify the limit or boundary on the distribution of different terms in the collection. Any term that occurs with a significantly high frequency is not going to be informative for us, and the barely present terms can undoubtedly be ignored and considered as noise. Some examples of stop words are *is*, *was*, *then*, and *the*.

Words that generally occur with high frequency and have no particular meaning are referred to as stop words. Words that occur just once or twice are more likely to be spelling errors or complicated words, and hence both these and stop words should not be considered for modeling the document in the **Term Document Matrix (TDM)**.

We will discuss a few dimensionality reduction techniques in brief and dive into their implementation using R.

Principal component analysis

Principal component analysis (PCA) reveals the internal structure of a dataset in a way that best explains the variance within the data. PCA identifies patterns to reduce the dimensions of the dataset without significant loss of information. The main aim of PCA is to project a high-dimensional feature space into a smaller subset to decrease computational cost. PCA helps in computing new features, which are called principal components; these principal components are uncorrelated linear combinations of the original features projected in the direction of higher variability. The important point is to map the set of features into a matrix, M, and compute the eigenvalues and eigenvectors. Eigenvectors provide simpler solutions to problems that can be modeled using linear transformations along axes by stretching, compressing, or flipping. Eigenvalues provide the length and magnitude of eigenvectors where such transformations occur. Eigenvectors with greater eigenvalues are selected in the new feature space because they enclose more information than eigenvectors with lower eigenvalues for a data distribution. The first principle component has the greatest possible variance, that is, the largest eigenvalues compared with the next principal component uncorrelated, relative to the first PC. The nth PC is the linear combination of the maximum variance that is uncorrelated with all previous PCs.

PCA comprises the following steps:

1. Compute the n-dimensional mean of the given dataset.
2. Compute the covariance matrix of the features.
3. Compute the eigenvectors and eigenvalues of the covariance matrix.

4. Rank/sort the eigenvectors by descending eigenvalue.
5. Choose x eigenvectors with the largest eigenvalues.

Eigenvector values represent the contribution of each variable to the principal component axis. Principal components are oriented in the direction of maximum variance in m-dimensional space.

PCA is one of the most widely used multivariate methods for discovering meaningful, new, informative, and uncorrelated features. This methodology also reduces dimensionality by rejecting low-variance features and is useful in reducing the computational requirements for classification and regression analysis.

Using R for PCA

R also has two inbuilt functions for accomplishing PCA: `prcomp()` and `princomp()`. These two functions expect the dataset to be organized with variables in columns and observations in rows and has a structure like a data frame. They also return the new data in the form of a data frame, and the principal components are given in columns.

`prcomp()` and `princomp()` are similar functions used for accomplishing PCA; they have a slightly different implementation for computing PCA. Internally, the `princomp()` function performs PCA using eigenvectors. The `prcomp()` function uses a similar technique known as **singular value decomposition (SVD)**. SVD has slightly better numerical accuracy, so `prcomp()` is generally the preferred function.

 `princomp()` fails in situations if the number of variables is larger than the number of observations.

Each function returns a list whose class is `prcomp()` or `princomp()`.

The information returned and terminology is summarized in the following table:

prcomp()	princomp()	Explanation
sdev	sdev	Standard deviation of each column
Rotations	Loading	Principle components
Center	Center	Subtracted value of each row or column to get the center data
Scale	Scale	Scale factors used
X	Score	The rotated data
	n.obs	Number of observations of each variable
	Call	The call to function that created the object

Here's a list of the functions available in different R packages for performing PCA:

- `PCA()`: FactoMineR package
- `acp()`: amap package
- `prcomp()`: stats package
- `princomp()`: stats package
- `dudi.pca()`: ade4 package
- `pcaMethods`: This package from Bioconductor has various convenient methods to compute PCA

Understanding the FactoMineR package

FactomineR is a R package that provides multiple functions for multivariate data analysis and dimensionality reduction. The functions provided in the package not only deals with quantitative data but also categorical data. Apart from PCA, correspondence and multiple correspondence analyses can also be performed using this package:

```
library(FactoMineR)
data<-replicate(10,rnorm(1000))
result.pca = PCA(data[,1:9], scale.unit=TRUE, graph=T)
print(result.pca)
```

Results for the principal component analysis (PCA).

The analysis was performed on 1,000 individuals, described by nine variables.

The results are available in the following objects:

Name	Description
$eig	Eigenvalues
$var	Results for the variables
varcoord	coord. for the variables
varcor	Correlations variables - dimensions
varcos2	cos2 for the variables
varcontrib	Contributions of the variables
$ind	Results for the individuals
indcoord	coord. for the individuals
indcos2	cos2 for the individuals
indcontrib	Contributions of the individuals

$call	Summary statistics
$call$centre	Mean of the variables
$call$ecart.type	Standard error of the variables
$call$row.w	Weights for the individuals
$call$col.w	Weights for the variables

Eigenvalue percentage of variance cumulative percentage of variance:

```
comp 1   1.1573559      12.859510          12.85951
comp 2   1.0991481      12.212757          25.07227
comp 3   1.0553160      11.725734          36.79800
comp 4   1.0076069      11.195632          47.99363
comp 5   0.9841510      10.935011          58.92864
comp 6   0.9782554      10.869505          69.79815
comp 7   0.9466867      10.518741          80.31689
comp 8   0.9172075      10.191194          90.50808
comp 9   0.8542724       9.491916         100.00000
```

Amap package

Amap is another package in the R environment that provides tools for clustering and PCA. It is an acronym for Another Multidimensional Analysis Package. One of the most widely used functions in this package is acp(), which does PCA on a data frame.

This function is akin to princomp() and prcomp(), except that it has slightly different graphic represention.

For more intricate details, refer to the CRAN-R resource page:

```
https://cran.r-project.org/web/packages/lLibrary(amap/amap.pdf
```

```
    Library(amap
    acp(data,center=TRUE,reduce=TRUE)
```

Additionally, weight vectors can also be provided as an argument. We can perform a robust PCA by using the `acpgen` function in the `amap` package:

```
acpgen(data,h1,h2,center=TRUE,reduce=TRUE,kernel="gaussien")
K(u,kernel="gaussien")
W(x,h,D=NULL,kernel="gaussien")
acprob(x,h,center=TRUE,reduce=TRUE,kernel="gaussien")
```

Proportion of variance

We look to construct components and to choose from them, the minimum number of components, which explains the variance of data with high confidence.

R has a `prcomp()` function in the base package to estimate principal components. Let's learn how to use this function to estimate the proportion of variance, eigen facts, and digits:

```
pca_base<-prcomp(data)
print(pca_base)
```

The `pca_base` object contains the standard deviation and rotations of the vectors. Rotations are also known as the principal components of the data. Let's find out the proportion of variance each component explains:

```
pr_variance<- (pca_base$sdev^2/sum(pca_base$sdev^2))*100
pr_variance
 [1] 11.678126 11.301480 10.846161 10.482861 10.176036  9.605907
9.498072
 [8]  9.218186  8.762572  8.430598
```

`pr_variance` signifies the proportion of variance explained by each component in descending order of magnitude.

Let's calculate the cumulative proportion of variance for the components:

```
cumsum(pr_variance)
 [1]  11.67813  22.97961  33.82577  44.30863  54.48467  64.09057
73.58864
 [8]  82.80683  91.56940 100.00000
```

Components 1-8 explain the 82% variance in the data.

Scree plot

If you wish to plot the variances against the number of components, you can use the `screeplot` function on the fitted model:

```
screeplot(pca_base)
```

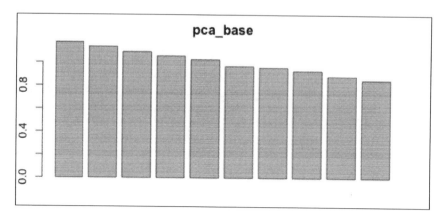

Reconstruction error

The components are estimated in such a way that the variance across each component is maximized while the reconstruction error is minimized. Reconstruction error in terms of PCA is the squared Euclidean distance between the actual data and its estimated equivalent. We intend to choose the orthonormal basis, which minimizes the error and the eigenvectors with minimum eigenvalues.

Can we reconstruct the original data, using the results of PCA?

```
loadings = t(pca_base$rotation[,1])
scores = pca_base$x[,1]
reconstruct_data = scores %*% loadings  + colMeans(data)
```

Correspondence analysis

Just like PCA, the basic idea behind correspondence analysis is to reduce the dimensionality of data and represent it in a low-dimensionality space. Correspondence analysis basically deals with contingency tables or cross tabs. This technique is designed to perform exploratory analysis on multi-way tables with some degree of correspondence between their dimensions. The common methodology followed for correspondence analysis involves the standardization of the cross tab table of frequencies so that the entries in the cross tab can be represented in terms of distance between the dimensions in a low-dimensional space.

There are a few packages available in R that provide efficient functions for correspondence analysis:

R functions	Package
ca()	ca
corresp(formula,nf,data)	MASS
dudi.coa(df, scannf = TRUE, nf = 2)	ade4
CA()	FactorMineR
afc()	amap

Let's look at an example application of the R functions for simple correspondence analysis:

```
# Load the package anacor to the session
library(anacor)
#Load dataset tocher , it s a frequency table
data(tocher)
resid<- anacor(tocher, scaling = c("standard", "centroid"))
print(resid)
```

CA fit:

Sum of eigenvalues: 0.2293315

Total chi-square value: 1240.039

Chi-Square decomposition

Chisq Proportion Cumulative Proportion:

Component 1   1073.331   0.866   0.866

Component 2   162.077   0.131   0.996

Component 3   4.630   0.004   1.000

Looking at the Chisquare decomposition, we can conclude that component 1 contributes to 86% of total inertia. Components 1 and 2 together are good enough to account for a significant percentage of inertia.

Let's run the Chisquare test of independence:

```
chisq.test(tocher)
```

Pearson's Chisquared test:

data: tocher

X-squared = 1240.039, df = 12, p-value < 2.2e-16

Let's visualize the joint and graph plots for the residuals:

```
plot(resid, plot.type = "jointplot", ylim = c(-1.5, 1.5))
plot(resid, plot.type = "graphplot", wlines = 5)
```

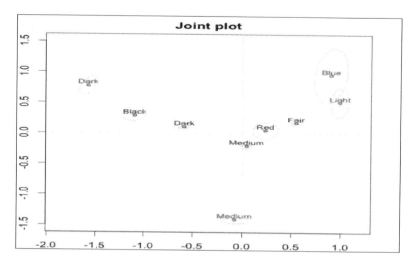

Other plotting options available in `amacor` are as follows:

- `regplot`: Frequency grid and regression line is plotted
- `transplot`: plot of initial to transformed/scaled data
- `benzplot`: plots the observed distance against fitted distance
- `rowplot`,`colplot`: plots row/column score separately

Canonical correspondence analysis

Canonical correspondence analysis (CCA) is different from PCA, as the relationships in PCA are linear. To explore the relationship between two multivariate set of variables, where we assume a cause-effect relation, we apply CCA. The qualitative variables are recorded as binary dummy variables for CCA and the fitted model provides a quantitative rescaling of the categorical variables:

```
library(ca)
data(bitterling)
data<-bitterling
```

```
total <- sum(data)
nrows <- nrow(data)
ncols <- ncol(data)
#dimensionality
a <- min(ncol(data)-1, nrow(data)-1)
labs<-c(1:a) #x- axis lables
# create the contingency table
data_matrix<-as.matrix(data)
# Add row column profile to contingency table
data_rowsum<-addmargins(data_matrix,1)
data_colsum<-addmargins(data_matrix,2)
# Apply average rule ,to get number of dimensions
col_dim<-round(100/(ncols-1), digits=1)
row_dim<-round(100/(nrows-1), digits=1)
thresh_dim<-(max(col_dim, row_dim))
data_ca<- summary(ca(data))
n_dim<- length(which(data_ca$scree[,3]>=thresh_dim))
# Malinvaud's Test
mal_ca<-CA(data, ncp=a, graph=FALSE)
mal_trow <- a
mal_tcol <- 6
mal_out <-matrix(ncol= mal_tcol, nrow=mal_trow)
names(mal_out) <- c("K", "Dimension", "Eigen value", "Chi-square",
"df", "p value")
mal_out[,1] <- c(0:(a-1))
mal_out[,2] <- c(1:a)
library(foreach)
library(doParallel)
cl <- makeCluster(4) # number of cores
registerDoParallel(cl)
foreach(i = 1:mal_trow) %dopar% {
  k <- -1+i
  mal_out[i,3] <- mal_ca$eig[i,1]
  mal_out[i,5] <- (nrows-k-1)*(ncols-k-1)
}
mal_out[,4] <- rev(cumsum(rev(mal_out[,3])))*total
mal_out[,6] <- round(pchisq(mal_out[,4], mal_out[,5], lower.
tail=FALSE), digits=6)
optimal.dimensionality <- length(which(mal_out[,6]<=0.05))
# plot bar chart of correlation between rows and columns, and add
reference line
dev.new()
perf_corr<-(1.0)
sqr.trace<-round(sqrt(sum(data_ca$scree[,2])), digits=3)
```

```
barplot(c(perf_corr, sqr.trace), main="Correlation coefficient between
rows & columns (=square root of the inertia)", sub="reference line:
threshold of important correlation ", ylab="correlation coeff.",
names.arg=c("correlation coeff. range", "correlation coeff. bt rows &
cols"), cex.main=0.80, cex.sub=0.80, cex.lab=0.80)
abline(h=0.20)
```

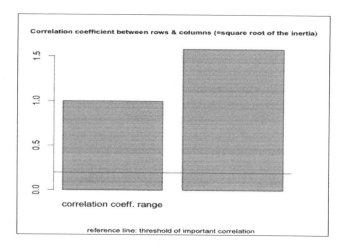

```
barplot(data_ca$scree[,3], xlab="Dimensions", ylab="% of Inertia",
names.arg=data_ca$scree[,1])
abline(h=thresh.sig.dim)
title (main="Percentage of inertia attributed to the dimensions",
sub="ref line: threshold of an optimal dimensionality of the solution,
according to the average rule", cex.main=0.80, cex.sub=0.80)
plot(mal_out[,6], type="o", xaxt="n", xlim=c(1, a), xlab="Dimensions",
ylab="p value")
axis(1, at=labs, labels=sprintf("%.0f",labs))
title(main="Malinvaud's test Plot", sub="dashed line: alpha 0.05
threshold", col.sub="RED", cex.sub=0.80)
abline(h=0.05, lty=2, col="RED")
```

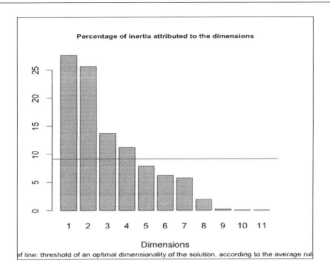

Percentage of inertia attributed to the dimensions

Dimensions

ef line: threshold of an optimal dimensionality of the solution, according to the average rul

```
userow_dimensionality <- 3
dims.to.be.plotted <- userow_dimensionality
# CA analysis by Greenacre's package to be used later on for the
Standard Biplots
res.ca <- ca(data, nd=dims.to.be.plotted)
str(res.ca)
List of 15
 $ sv       : num [1:11] 0.831 0.799 0.585 0.529 0.443 ...
 $ nd       : num 3
 $ rownames : chr [1:12] "jk" "tu" "hb" "chs" ...
 $ rowmass  : num [1:12] 0.1748 0.0382 0.1021 0.0709 0.0853 ...
 $ rowdist  : num [1:12] 1.19 1.01 1.02 1.31 2.69 ...
 $ rowinertia: num [1:12] 0.2466 0.0386 0.1064 0.1214 0.6195 ...
 $ rowcoord : num [1:12, 1:3] -0.04047 -0.00192 0.16761 0.20569
-3.12697 ...
 $ rowsup   : logi(0)
 $ colnames : chr [1:12] "jk" "tu" "hb" "chs" ...
 $ colmass  : num [1:12] 0.1983 0.0101 0.1167 0.0792 0.0864 ...
 $ coldist  : num [1:12] 1.159 0.798 1.075 1.191 2.677 ...
 $ colinertia: num [1:12] 0.26613 0.00644 0.13485 0.11225 0.6189 ...
 $ colcoord : num [1:12, 1:3] -0.0126 0.0104 0.1632 0.2324 -3.113 ...
 $ colsup   : logi(0)
 $ call     : language ca.matrix(obj = as.matrix(obj), nd = ..1)
 - attr(*, "class")= chr "ca"
# CA output as dataframe to be used for the some graphs to come
cadataframe<-summary(ca(data, nd=dims.to.be.plotted))
# plot the quality of the display of categories on successive pairs of
dimensions
```

```
#row categories
dev.new()
counter <- 1
for(i in seq(9, ncol(cadataframe$rows), 3)){
  counter <- counter +1
  quality.rows <- (cadataframe$rows[,6]+cadataframe$rows[,i])/10
  barplot(quality.rows, ylim=c(0,100), xlab="Row categories",
ylab=paste("Quality of the display (% of inertia) on Dim. 1+",
counter), names.arg=cadataframe$rows[,1], cex.lab=0.80)
}
```

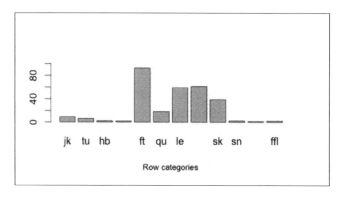

```
#column categories
dev.new()
counter <- 1
for(i in seq(9, ncol(cadataframe$columns), 3)){
  counter <- counter +1
  quality.cols <- (cadataframe$columns[,6]+cadataframe$columns[,i])/10
  barplot(quality.cols, ylim=c(0,100), xlab="Column categories",
ylab=paste("Quality of the display (% of inertia) on Dim. 1+",
counter), names.arg=cadataframe$columns[,1], cex.lab=0.80)
}
# charts of categories contribution
# plot bar charts of contribution of row categories to the axes, and
add a reference line
dev.new()
counter <- 0
for(i in seq(7, ncol(cadataframe$rows), 3)){
  counter <- counter +1
  barplot(cadataframe$rows[,i], ylim=c(0,1000), xlab="Row categories",
ylab=paste("Contribution to Dim. ",counter," (in permills)"), names.
arg=cadataframe$rows[,1], cex.lab=0.80)
  abline(h=round(((100/nrows)*10), digits=0))
}
```

```
# plot bar charts of contribution of column categories to the axes,
and add a reference line
dev.new()
counter <- 0
for(i in seq(7, ncol(cadataframe$columns), 3)){
  counter <- counter +1
  barplot(cadataframe$columns[,i], ylim=c(0,1000), xlab="Column
categories", ylab=paste("Contribution to Dim. ",counter," (in
permills)"), names.arg=cadataframe$columns[,1], cex.lab=0.80)
  abline(h=round(((100/ncols)*10), digits=0))
}
# let us estimate the correlation of categories to dimensions
# row categories
dev.new()
counter <- 0
for(i in seq(6, ncol(cadataframe$rows), 3)){
  counter <- counter +1
  correl.rows <- round(sqrt((cadataframe$rows[,i]/1000)), digits=3)
  barplot(correl.rows, ylim=c(0,1), xlab="Row categories",
ylab=paste("Correlation with Dim. ", counter), names.
arg=cadataframe$rows[,1], cex.lab=0.80)
}
#column categories
dev.new()
counter <- 0
for(i in seq(6, ncol(cadataframe$columns), 3)){
  counter <- counter +1
  correl.cols <- round(sqrt((cadataframe$columns[,i]/1000)), digits=3)
  barplot(correl.cols, ylim=c(0,1), xlab="Column categories",
ylab=paste("Correlation with Dim. ", counter), names.
arg=cadataframe$columns[,1], cex.lab=0.80)
}
  #let us check the Contingency Table
print(addmargins(data_matrix))
# Association coefficients can be estimated by
library(vcd)
print(assocstats(data_matrix))
                    X^2  df P(> X^2)
Likelihood Ratio 9251 121         0
Pearson                14589 121          0
Phi-Coefficient: 1.581
Contingency Coeff.: 0.845
Cramer's V       : 0.477
```

Pearson's Chi-squared test

```
#Chi-square test
print(chisq.test(data))
X-squared = 14589.07, df = 121, p-value < 2.2e-16
#Total Inertia
print(sum(cadataframe$scree[,2]))
[1] 2.499841
# Square root of the Total Inertia
print(sqr.trace)
[1] 1.581
# Correspondence Analysis summary
print(cadataframe)

Principal inertias (eigenvalues):
 dim    value      %    cum%   scree plot
  1     0.689905  27.6  27.6   *************************
  2     0.639174  25.6  53.2   ***********************
  3     0.342155  13.7  66.9   ************
  4     0.280273  11.2  78.1   **********
  5     0.196284   7.9  85.9   *******
  6     0.154954   6.2  92.1   ******
  7     0.142684   5.7  97.8   *****
  8     0.048760   2.0  99.8   **
  9     0.005384   0.2 100.0
 10     0.000232   0.0 100.0
 11     3.5e-050   0.0 100.0
        --------  -----
 Total: 2.499841 100.0
```

Multiple correspondence analysis

Multiple correspondence analysis is methodology to establish the association between multiple discrete categorical or qualitative variables. This makes it different from simple correspondence analysis, which accounts for association between only two categorical variables. It is a compelling statistical tool used for allocating scores to subjects and sets for multiple categorical variables. Multiple correspondence analyses are categorized by the optimal scaling of categorical variables. This analysis is considered as a categorical equivalent of PCA, a form of non-linear principal component analysis. It is also seen as multidimensional scaling of matrices. Multiple correspondence analyses have been chosen by many academic fields to analyze huge amount of survey data.

This technique provides the association between two or more categorical variables. The data can be represented graphically in a highly informative and intuitive way using this technique. One of the distinctive features of correspondence analysis is the ways in which one can derive the basic simultaneous equations. These equations are related to the Pearson's chi-squared statistic and also to the different methods of quantification. The association between the variables of a two-way contingency table may be considered a special case of multiple correspondence analyses.

The scaling in multiple correspondence analyses can be performed by the following methods:

- Generalized SVD
- Least-squares algorithms and alternating least squares
- Eigen-decomposition

There are different variations of multiple correspondence analysis:

- Stacking and concatenation
- Joint correspondence analysis
- Ordered multiple correspondence analysis

MCA functions	Package
`mca()`	MCA
`MCA()`	FactomineR
`dudi.acm()`	ade4
`homals()`	homals
`Mica()`	ca

Singular vector decomposition (SVD) is a dimensionality reduction technique that gained a lot of popularity in recent times after the famous Netflix Movie Recommendation challenge. Since its inception, it has found its usage in many applications in statistics, mathematics, and signal processing.

It is primarily a technique to factorize any matrix; it can be real or a complex matrix. A rectangular matrix can be factorized into two orthonormal matrices and a diagonal matrix of positive real values. An *m*n* matrix is considered as m points in n-dimensional space; SVD attempts to find the best k dimensional subspace that fits the data:

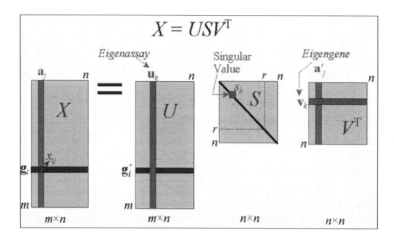

SVD in R is used to compute approximations of singular values and singular vectors of large-scale data matrices. These approximations are made using different types of memory-efficient algorithm, and IRLBA is one of them (named after Lanczos bi-diagonalization (IRLBA) algorithm). We shall be using the irlba package here in order to implement SVD.

Implementation of SVD using R

The following code will show the implementation of SVD using R:

```
# List of packages for the session
packages = c("foreach", "doParallel", "irlba")
# Install CRAN packages (if not already installed)
inst <- packages %in% installed.packages()
if(length(packages[!inst]) > 0) install.packages(packages[!inst])
# Load packages into session
lapply(packages, require, character.only=TRUE)
# register the parallel session for
registerDoParallel(cores=detectCores(all.tests=TRUE))
std_svd <- function(x, k, p=25, iter=0 1 ) {
m1 <- as.matrix(x)
r <- nrow(m1)
c <- ncol(m1)
```

```
p <- min( min(r,c)-k,p)
z <- k+p
m2 <- matrix ( rnorm(z*c), nrow=c, ncol=z)
y <- m1 %*% m2
q <- qr.Q(qr(y))
b<- t(q) %*% m1
#iterations
b1<-foreach( i=i1:iter ) %dopar% {
  y1 <- m1 %*% t(b)
  q1 <- qr.Q(qr(y1))
  b1 <- t(q1) %*% m1
}
b1<-b1[[iter]]
b2 <- b1 %*% t(b1)
eigens <- eigen(b2, symmetric=T)
result <- list()
result$svalues <- sqrt(eigens$values)[1:k]
u1=eigens$vectors[1:k,1:k]
result$u <- (q %*% eigens$vectors)[,1:k]
result$v <- (t(b) %*% eigens$vectors %*% diag(1/eigens$values))[,1:k]
return(result)
}
svd<- std_svd(x=data,k=5))
# singular vectors
svd$svalues
[1] 35.37645 33.76244 32.93265 32.72369 31.46702
```

We obtain the following values after running SVD using the IRLBA algorithm:

- d: approximate singular values.
- u: nu approximate left singular vectors
- v: nv approximate right singular vectors
- iter: # of IRLBA algorithm iterations
- mprod: # of matrix vector products performed

These values can be used for obtaining results of SVD and understanding the overall statistics about how the algorithm performed.

Latent factors

```
# svd$u, svd$v
dim(svd$u)   #u value after running IRLBA
[1] 1000    5
dim(svd$v)   #v value after running IRLBA
[1] 10   5
```

A modified version of the previous function can be achieved by altering the power iterations for a robust implementation:

```
foreach( i = 1:iter )%dopar% {
  y1 <- m1 %*% t(b)
  y2 <- t(y1) %*% y1
  r2 <- chol(y2, pivot = T)
  q1 <- y2 %*% solve(r2)
  b1 <- t(q1) %*% m1
}
b2 <- b1 %*% t(b1)
```

Some other functions available in R packages are as follows:

Functions	Package
svd()	svd
Irlba()	irlba
svdImpute	bcv

ISOMAP – moving toward non-linearity

ISOMAP is a nonlinear dimension reduction method and is representative of isometric mapping methods. ISOMAP is one of the approaches for manifold learning. ISOMAP finds the map that preserves the global, nonlinear geometry of the data by preserving the geodesic manifold inter-point distances. Like multi-dimensional scaling, ISOMAP creates a visual presentation of distance of a number of objects. Geodesic is the shortest curve along the manifold connecting two points induced by a neighborhood graph. Multi-dimensional scaling uses the Euclidian distance measure; since the data is in a nonlinear format, ISOMPA uses geodesic distance. ISOMAP can be viewed as an extension of metric multi-dimensional scaling.

At a very high level, ISOMAP can be describes in four steps:

1. Determine the neighbor of each point
2. Construct a neighborhood graph
3. Compute the shortest distance path between all pairs

4. Construct k-dimensional coordinate vectors by applying MDS

Geodesic distance approximation is basically calculated in three ways:

- **Neighboring points**: Input-space distance
- **Faraway points**: A sequence of short hops between neighboring points
- **Method**: Finding shortest paths in a graph with edges connecting neighboring data points

```
source("http://bioconductor.org/biocLite.R")
biocLite("RDRToolbox")
library('RDRToolbox')
swiss_Data=SwissRoll(N = 1000, Plot=TRUE)
x=SwissRoll()
open3d()
plot3d(x, col=rainbow(1050)[-c(1:50)],box=FALSE,type="s",size=1)
```

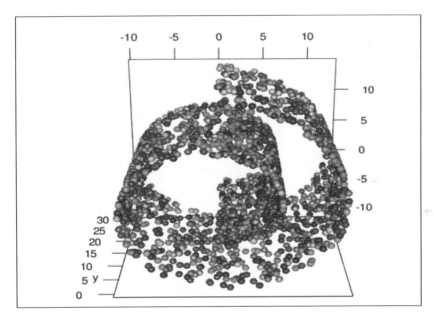

```
simData_Iso = Isomap(data=swiss_Data, dims=1:10,
k=10,plotResiduals=TRUE)
```

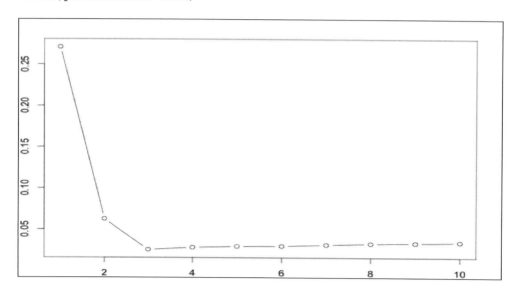

```
library(vegan)data(BCI)
distance <- vegdist(BCI)
tree <- spantree(dis)
pl1 <- ordiplot(cmdscale(dis), main="cmdscale")
lines(tree, pl1, col="red")
z <- isomap(distance, k=3)
rgl.isomap(z, size=4, color="red")
pl2 <- plot(isomap(distance, epsilon=0.5), main="isomap epsilon=0.5")
pl3 <- plot(isomap(distance, k=5), main="isomap k=5")
pl4 <- plot(z, main="isomap k=3")
```

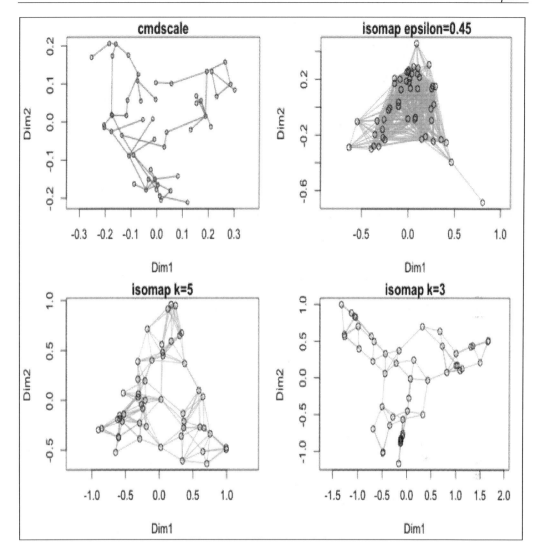

Summary

The idea of this chapter was to get you familiar with some of the generic dimensionality reduction methods and their implementation using R language. We discussed a few packages that provide functions to perform these tasks. We also covered a few custom functions that can be utilized to perform these tasks. Kudos, you have completed the basics of text mining with R. You must be feeling confident about various data mining methods, text mining algorithms (related to natural language processing of the texts) and after reading this chapter, dimensionality reduction.

If you feel a little low on confidence, do not be upset. Turn a few pages back and try implementing those tiny code snippets on your own dataset and figure out how they help you understand your data.

Remember this - to mine something, you have to get into it by yourself. This holds true for text as well.

5
Text Summarization and Clustering

High dimensional unstructured data comes with the great trouble of organizing, querying, and information retrieval. If we can learn how to extract latent thematic structure in a text document or a collection of such documents, we can harness the wealth of information that can be retrieved; something that would not have been feasible without the advancements in natural language processing methodologies. In this chapter, we will learn about topic modeling and text summarization. We will learn how to extract hidden themes from documents and collections in order to be able to effectively use it for dozens of purposes such as corpus summarization, document organization, document classification, taxonomy generation of web documents, organizing search engine query results, news or article recommendation systems, and duplicate content detection. We will also discuss an interesting application of probabilistic language models in sentence completion:

- Topic modeling
- Latent semantic analysis
- Machine learning-based text summarization
- Text clustering
- Sentence completion

Topic modeling

Topic models can be used for discovering the underlying themes or topics that are present in an unstructured collection of documents. The collection of documents can be organized based on the discovered topics, so that users can easily browse through the documents based on topics of their interest. There are various topic modeling algorithms that can be applied to a collection of documents to achieve this. Clustering is a very useful technique used to group documents, but this doesn't always fit the requirements. When we cluster a text document, the results in each text exclusively belong to exactly one cluster. Let's consider this scenario: We have a book called *Text Mining with R Programming Language*. Should this book be grouped with R programming-related books, or with text mining-related books? The book is about R programming as well as text mining, and thus should be listed in both sections. In this topic, we will learn methods that do not cluster documents into completely separate groups, but allow each document to refer to several topics. These topics will be identified automatically from a collection of text documents. The field of machine learning that deals with these problems is called topic modeling. What does a document signify? What are the themes that can be ascribed to? A collection of social media articles can relate to multiple different themes, such as business, fashion, and sports. If given a task of organizing or querying a large collection of document corpuses, topic modeling is a tool that comes in handy.

Let's briefly discuss the two common topic models:

- **Latent Dirichlet Allocation (LDA)**
- **Correlated Topic Model (CTM)**

Latent Dirichlet Allocation

Latent Dirichlet Allocation (LDA) is one of the most widely used topic modeling methods, which belongs to a class of models that are called **generative models**. There are latent themes present in every document, and each word in the document contributes to the theme or topic, which encodes our assumption about the document or collection. If we can effectively group documents with similar underlying topics and themes, we can solve the trivial issues in searching, organizing, and summarizing huge archives of unstructured data. We uncover the latent topics pervading the collection of documents and annotate the documents according to the topics discovered, which is utilized to extract context, summarize, or organize the collection. The idea behind LDA is that we assume a fixed number of topics are distributed over the documents in the whole collection:

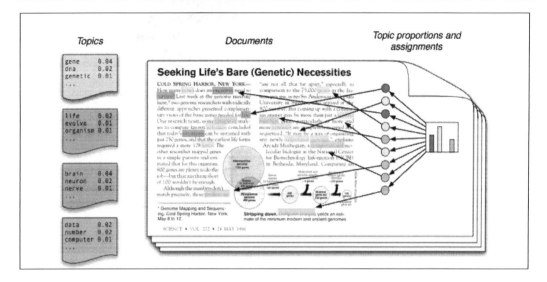

The image is vital to this topic and similar image needs to be generated, as it is a copied image from web.

Each document is an amalgamation of multiple topics across the corpus; each topic is an assortment of thousands of words, while each word is an entity that contributes to the theme of the document. Still, we only can observe a document as a whole; everything else is hidden. Probabilistic models of topic modeling have the objective to dissect documents to extract those latent features, which can help summarize a document or organize a group of them.

Topic modeling adopts a three-pronged strategy to tackle the complexity of extracting themes from the collection of documents:

- Every word in each document is assigned a topic
- The proportion of each unique topic is estimated for every document
- For every corpus, the topic distribution is explored

The topic labeled to an observed word depends on a posterior, which takes into account the topic and proportion parameters defined, and the assignment of topics to each word in a document, as well as to each document in a corpus. The topic can be assumed to be a probability distribution across the multitude of words, while the topic models are nothing but a probabilistic relationship between the latent unobserved themes and faction of observed linguistic variables. LDA is a model that imbibes this process. This model randomly generates observable data values based on some hidden parameters and follows a generative process; in this process we estimate the joint probability distribution of all the variables. We calculate the probability weights for words, and create the topics based on the weight of each word; each topic will assign different weights to different words. For this model, the order of the words does not matter as it will treat each document as a bag of words - this assumption may not be the best, since the sequence of the words in the sentence are lost. The order of the documents also does not matter. This type of language simplification is very rudimentary and often works because it still helps us to understand the semantics of the topics; knowing which words were used in a document and their frequencies makes it good enough to make decisions on which topic they belong to.

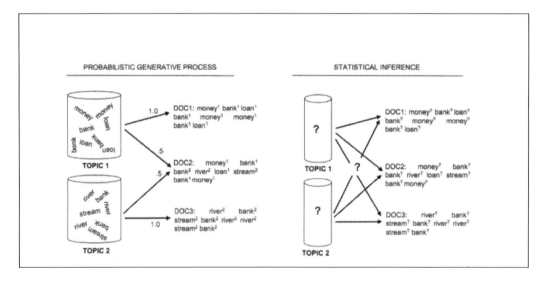

```
install.packages("topicmodels")
install.packages("tm")
library(topicmodels)
library(tm)
```

For understanding topic modeling we will be using the NYTimes dataset. The dataset is arranged in five columns, such as Article_ID, Date, Title, Subject Topic, and Code - it has 3,104 rows of data. This dataset contains headlines from NYTimes articles. We will choose a random sample of 500 articles for the purposes of our example and understanding:

```
data(NYTimes)
```

Let's use the sample function from R base package - this function takes a sample of the specified size from the input elements either with or without replacement. After execution of the preceding statement, NYTimesData will have 500 random samples of data in its data frame:

```
NYTimesData <- NYTimes[sample(1:3104,size=500,replace=FALSE),]
```

1. If we inspect the data frame, we have two text columns, title and subject:

   ```
   head(NYTimesData , 5)
   Article_ID Date       TitleSubject      Topic.Code
   28096      10-May-01   Horse Racing; Mystery Illness Hurts Horse
   Breeding in Kentucky          fungus believed to be cause of
   stillborn foal births in Kentucky 4
   42085      1-Apr-96   POLITICS: IN CONGRESS; The Speaker's Gruff
   No. 2 Takes Charge in the House   dick armey       20
   ```

2. Let's combine the data from both the columns into a variable for processing:

   ```
   Textdata <- cbind(as.vector(NYTimesData$Title),as.
   vector(NYTimesData$Subject));
   ```

3. Now we will convert it to character class by passing the text data into an `apply` function:

   ```
   TestData <- apply(as.matrix(Textdata), 1, paste, collapse = " ")
   ```

4. Here we are converting the test data to UTF8 character encoding:

   ```
   TestData <- sapply(as.vector(TestData, mode = "character"), iconv,
   to = "UTF8", sub = "byte")
   ```

5. Now let's create a `Corpus` from the data so that we can run various pre-processing steps on it:

   ```
   corpus <- Corpus(VectorSource(TestData), readerControl =
   list(language = 'english'))
   ```

6. As explained in the previous chapters, we will do various pre-processing steps on the text data before analyzing it as shown here:

    ◦ Remove punctuation

    ◦ Remove numbers

    ◦ Remove stop words

    ◦ Strip out white spaces

    ◦ Stem words

```
control <- list(bounds = list(local = c(1, Inf)), language =
'english', tolower = TRUE, removeNumbers = TRUE, removePunctuation =
TRUE, stopwords = TRUE, stripWhitespace = TRUE,  stemWords=wordStem ,
wordLengths = c(3,20), weighting = weightTf)
```

Now, we will create the `DocumentTermMatrix` and pass our list of pre-processing actions that have to be performed on our corpus. We can also remove the sparse terms from the matrix if need be:

```
matrix <- DocumentTermMatrix(corpus, control = control)
```

For LDA the number of topics must be fixed before modeling; we have to identify the number of topics in our dataset. The `NYTimes` dataset has already been classified. We can simply use a `unique()` function to determine the number of unique topics:

```
numberOfTopics <- length(unique(NYTimesData$Topic.Code))
```

Now, let's generate the LDA model based on the two inputs, `numberOfTopics` and `DocumentTermMatrix`:

```
lda <- LDA(matrix, numberOfTopics)

terms(lda)
```

Topic 1   Topic 2   Topic 3   Topic 4   Topic 5   Topic 6   Topic 7   Topic 8   Topic 9   Topic 10   Topic 11   Topic 12

"end"   "program"   "crisis"   "kerry"   "budget"   "scandal"   "bush"   "court"   "president"   "schools"   "suicide"   "iraq"

Topic 13   Topic 14   Topic 15   Topic 16   Topic 17   Topic 18   Topic 19   Topic 20   Topic 21   Topic 22   Topic 23   Topic 24

"special"   "new"   "bill"   "census"   "sars"   "time"   "war" "microsoft"   "day"   "iraq"   "bush"   "oil"

Topic 25   Topic 26   Topic 27

"campaign"   "bush"   "ground"

Correlated topic model

As the name of the model suggests, this way of modeling collections helps us understand the correlation between the hidden topics in the collection of documents. This technique is very useful when we have to understand the relationship between each topic and build graphs about the topics, or build a topic of interest or document browser. This will help the user in navigating through the collection of documents by their topics of interest or preference, and ease their experience in finding the right content from a huge set of documents. An LDA model sets the basic principles for topic modeling and correlated topic modeling is an extension of this, building upon the LDA model. As explained in the previous section, an LDA model does not take into account the order in which the words occur or whether the order of the words is lost or is exchangeable. LDA is a high dimensional vector model - in LDA, the assumption is that the occurrence of one topic is not correlated to another topic; for example, an LDA fails to directly model correlation between topics, whereas a **Correlated topic model** (**CTM**) is a hierarchical model. A CTM provides better insights about the data, which helps in better visualization. A CTM models the words of each document from document-specific random variables, and can capture the diversity in grouped data that illustrates multiple hidden patterns. A CTM gives better predictive performance, but comes at the expense of extra computation cost.

For both models; LDA and CTM, the number of topics has to be fixed before modeling a corpus; they follow a generative process:

- Determine term distribution for each topic
- Determine proportions of the topic distribution for the document
- For each word choose a topic, then choose a word conditioned on that topic

This is the list of steps followed in topic modeling:

1. The provided data can be in various formats. Creating a corpus or vocabulary out of the given data is the first step.
2. Process the created corpus to remove noisy data. This involves:
   ° Tokenizing
   ° Stemming
   ° Stop word removal
   ° Removing numbers
   ° Removing punctuation
   ° Removing terms below certain length
   ° Converting to lower case

3. Create the document term matrix of the processed corpus.

4. Remove the sparse entries from the document term matrix.

5. This matrix can be provided as the input to LDA and CTM.

Model selection

Selecting the number of topics is a tricky problem; for fitting a given document-term matrix using the LDA model or the CTM, the number of topics needs to be fixed before modeling. There are various approaches to select the number of topics:

- Generally the number of topics is not known, but we can run the models on a different number of topics and find the best value in a data-driven way

- Bayesian approach

- Hierarchical Dirichlet process

- Cross validation on likelihood approach

R Package for topic modeling

We use the `topicmodels` package for topic modeling. This package provides an interface to the C code for LDA models and CTM, and C++ code for fitting LDA models using Gibbs sampling.

The main functions in package topic models for fitting the LDA and CTM models are `LDA()` and `CTM()`, respectively. These two functions have the same arguments. The functions are as shown in the following code:

```
LDA(x, k, method = "VEM", control = NULL, model = NULL ...)
CTM(x, k, method = "VEM", control = NULL, model = NULL ...)
```

Fitting the LDA model with the VEM algorithm

The following arguments are possible for the control list:

```
control_LDA_VEM<-  list( estimate.alpha = TRUE, alpha = 50/k,
estimate.beta = TRUE,verbose = 0, prefix = tempfile(), save = 0, keep
= 0, seed = as.integer(Sys.time()), nstart = 1, best = TRUE,var =
list(iter.max = 500, tol = 10^-6),em = list(iter.max = 1000, tol =
10^-4),initialize = "random")
```

For more information about function parameters, refer to the package documentation.

Latent semantic analysis

Latent Semantic Analysis (LSA) is a modeling technique that can be used to understand a given collection of documents. It also provides us with insights into the relationship between words in the documents, unravels the concealed structure in the document contents, and creates a group of suitable topics - each topic has information about the data variation that explains the context of the corpus. This modeling technique can come in handy in a variety of natural language processing or information retrieval tasks. LSA can filter out the noise features in the data and represent the data in a simpler form, and discover topics with high affinity.

The topics that are extracted from the collection of documents have the following properties:

- The amount of similarity each topic has with each document in the corpus.

- The amount of similarity each topic has with each term in the corpus.

- It also provides a significance score that highlights the importance of the topic and the variance in the data set.

- LSA uses a linear algebra technique called **singular value decomposition (SVD)**. LSA deduces a lower-dimensional representation of vectors from high dimensional space. The input to the LSA model is a term-document matrix that is generated from the corpus using word frequencies - each column corresponds to a document and each row corresponds to terms. SVD then factorizes this matrix into three matrices: the first matrix expresses topics in regard to documents, the second matrix expresses topics in regard to terms and the third matrix contains the importance for each topic.

SVD allows us to obtain a low dimensional vector from a high dimensional vector with minimum loss of precision.

R Package for latent semantic analysis

We are going to use the `lsa` package for latent semantic analysis. The package supports methods for dimensionality calculation, term weighting, triple binding, and correlation measurement. It provides a high-level abstraction to core API's `lsa()`, `fold_in()` `as.textmatrix()`, `query()`, `textmatrix()` functions.

Illustrative example of LSA

1. First, we will install the required libraries:

```
install.packages("ggplot2")
install.packages("lsa")
install.packages("tm")
```

2. Next, we will load the libraries:

```
library(tm)
library(ggplot2)
library(lsa)
```

3. We need to make up data to apply LSA, so let's create a corpus; I have randomly selected and made up nine titles of books related to investment:

```
InvestingMantra<- c(
     "Little Guide to Stock Market Investing.",
     "Investing For Dummies, 4th Edition.",
     "Guarantee Your Stock Market Returns.",
     "The Little Book of Value Investing.",
     "Value of Investing: From Paul",
     "Rich Dad's Guide to Investing: What the Rich Invest in, That
      the Poor and the Middle Class Do Not!",
     "Investing in Real Estate, 5th Edition.",
     "Stock Investing For Dummies.",
    "The ABC's of Real Estate Investing"
 )
```

4. Let's have an index for each title of the book, which will help us in plotting graphs - let's create `factor` as follows:

```
view <- factor(rep(c("T1", "T2", "T3","T4", "T5", "T6","T7", "T8",
"T9"), each = 1))
```

5. We will create a `DataFrame` from the `character` class:

```
IM_DataFrame<- data.frame(InvestingMantra, view, stringsAsFactors
= FALSE)
```

6. For the purpose of analysis, we need to convert the data frame into a `Corpus` object:

```
investingMantra_corpus<- Corpus(VectorSource(IM_
DataFrame$InvestingMantra))

inspect(investingMantra_corpus)
```

7. We now need to pre-process the corpus, convert text to lower-case, perform stemming, remove numbers, remove punctuation characters, and remove stop words:

```
investingMantra_corpus<- tm_map(investingMantra_corpus, tolower)
investingMantra_corpus<- tm_map(investingMantra_corpus,
removePunctuation)
investingMantra_corpus<- tm_map(investingMantra_corpus,
removeNumbers)
investingMantra_corpus<- tm_map(investingMantra_corpus,
function(x) removeWords(x, stopwords("english")))
investingMantra_corpus<- tm_map(investingMantra_corpus,
stemDocument, language = "english")
investingMantra_corpus<- tm_map(investingMantra_corpus,
PlainTextDocument)
```

8. Inspect the `corpus` after cleansing:

```
inspect(investingMantra_corpus)
```

9. Find the `TermDocumentMatrix`:

```
investingMantra_TD_Matrix<- as.matrix(TermDocumentMatrix(investing
Mantra_corpus))
```

10. Calculate a weighted document-term matrix according to the chosen local and/or global weighting scheme:

```
investingMantra_TD_Matrix.lsa<- lw_bintf(investingMantra_TD_
Matrix) * gw_idf(investingMantra_TD_Matrix)
```

11. Calculate the latent semantic space for the give document-term matrix and create `lsaSpace`:

```
lsaSpace<- lsa(investingMantra_TD_Matrix.lsa)
```

12. Compute the distance matrix:

```
distnce_matrix_lsa<- dist(t(as.textmatrix(lsaSpace)))
distnce_matrix_lsa
```

13. Let's start to plot the distance matrix:

```
fit<- cmdscale(distnce_matrix_lsa , eig = TRUE, k = 2)
points<- data.frame(x = fit$points[, 1], y = fit$points[, 2])
ggplot(points, aes(x = x, y = y)) + geom_point(data = points,
aes(x = x, y = y,size=5, color = IM_DataFrame$view)) + geom_
text(data = points, aes(x = x, y = y - 0.2, label = row.names(IM_
DataFrame)))
```

14. The following figure shows the plot of titles; we can clearly see the cluster of titles:

   ° T1, and T3 talk about Stock Market

   ° T7, and T9 talk about Real Estate

   ° T2, T4, T5, and T8 talk about investing

   ° T6 is an outlier

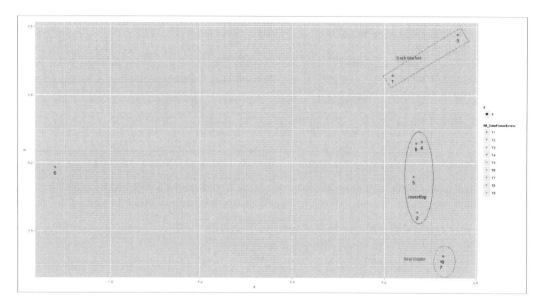

Text clustering

Text clustering is an unsupervised learning algorithm that helps to find and group similar objects together. The objective is to create groups or clusters that are internally coherent but are substantially dissimilar from each other, or they are far from each other when we express similarity in terms of distance. In simple words, the objects inside a cluster are as similar to each other, as possible, while the objects in one cluster are as dissimilar or far from the objects in another cluster as possible.

Traditionally, clustering has been applied on numeric data. Lately, it has found its usage even in text data. Text clustering is utilized to group text objects of different granularities such as documents, paragraphs, sentences, or terms together. We can find the application of text clustering in many tasks related to text data, for example, corpus summarization, document organization, document classification, taxonomy generation of web documents, organizing search engine query results, news or article recommendation systems, and duplicate content detection.

There are general purpose unsupervised learning algorithms that work well on numeric data and have also been widely used in text clustering. K-means and hierarchical clustering algorithms are among the most popular examples.

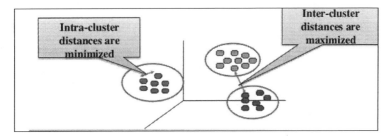

Document clustering

Document clustering is the process of grouping or partitioning text documents into meaningful groups. The hypothesis of the clustering algorithm is based on minimizing the distance between objects in a cluster, while keeping the intra-cluster distance at maximum.

For example, if we have a collection of news articles and we perform clustering on the collection, we will find that the similar documents are closer to each other and lie in the same cluster.

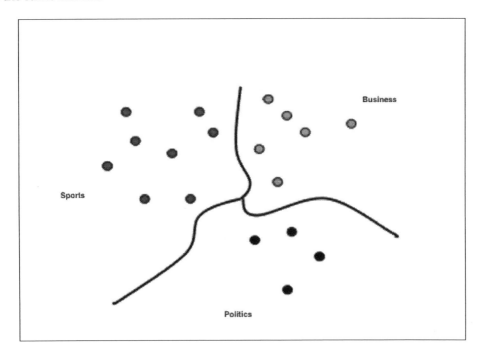

Some of the commonly used texts clustering methods are as follows:

- Standard methods:
  - K-means
  - Hierarchical clustering

- Specialized clustering:
  - Suffix tree clustering
  - Frequent-term set-based

Let's take a simple example of a term document matrix created from data available with tm package in R:

```
library(tm)
data("crude")
dtm<- DocumentTermMatrix(crude,control = list(weighting =
function(x)
weightTfIdf(x, normalize =
FALSE),
stopwords = TRUE))
dtm
<<DocumentTermMatrix (documents: 20, terms: 1200)>>
Non-/sparse entries: 1890/22110
Sparsity: 92%
Maximal term length: 17
Weighting: term frequency - inverse document frequency (tf-idf)
# Remove sparse terms
dtm<- removeSparseTerms(dtm,sparse=0.90)
<<DocumentTermMatrix (documents: 20, terms: 336)>>
Non-/sparse entries: 1028/5692
Sparsity: 85%
Maximal term length: 14
Weighting: term frequency - inverse document frequency (tf-idf)
dtm_tx<- weightTfIdf(dtm)
mat_dtm<- as.matrix(dtm_tx)
rownames(mat_dtm) <- 1:nrow(mat_dtm)
# Term Normalization
normalise_dtm<- function(y) y/apply(y, MARGIN=1, FUN=function(k)
sum(k^2)^.5)
dtm_norm<- normalise_dtm(mat_dtm)
cl<- kmeans(dtm_norm, 8)
cl
# Check the number of objects in each cluster
table(cl$cluster)
```

Available components in the k-means object are:

cluster, centers, totss, withinss, tot.withinss, betweenss, size, iter, and ifault.

```
# Check the cluster assigned to each object
cl$cluster
# check the center of each clusters
cl$centers
# Within cluster sum of squares by cluster
cl$withinss
### Cluster visualisation using 2 principal components
plot(prcomp(m_norm)$x, col=cl$cl)
```

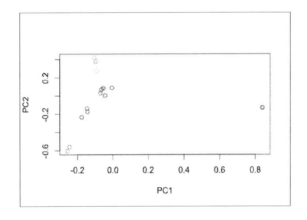

```
## hierarchical clustering
library(proxy)
### Complexity (O(n^2))
distance<- dist(dtm_norm, method="cosine")
hc<- hclust(distance, method="average")
plot(hc)
```

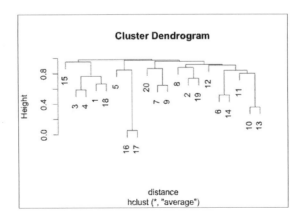

```
group_clust<- cutree(hc, k=5) # cut tree into 5 clusters
# drawdendogram with red borders around the 5 clusters
rect.hclust(hc, k=5, border="red")
```

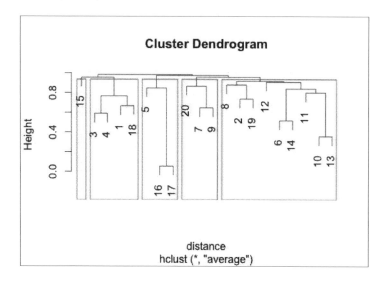

Feature selection for text clustering

The application of text clustering technologies is becoming predominant. Text clustering has been embraced by many industries, such as bio-medical, defense, telecommunication, and Internet companies, to solve various challenges, understand customer behavior, and understand trending news. Some of the applications are spam classification in e-mails, clustering news articles based on user interest, content management and document categorization, customer support applications, call log categorization, and capturing issue trends. The main challenge in text classification is the high dimensionality of feature space and the high degree of class imbalance. Feature selection is the process of creating a subset of terms that can be used for text classification. The goal of feature selection is to improve the classification model's efficiency and accuracy, and eliminate noisy features. Feature selection can be modest or aggressive. The fewer features selected, the more aggressive the feature selection method. Feature selection has a high reduction factor, and the number of available features are highly reduced.

In the context of text classification, the words or terms make up the features - for good classification or clustering, we need good features. Good features contain useful/vital information that the classifiers can use to decide the category of the document. Poor quality features contain less information, such as stop words. We need to remove these irrelevant features for efficiency of classifier performance.

Feature selection is an important step in text categorization and classifications, and there are various methods used to reduce the document vector, that is, reduce the dimensionality of the text document. Let's look into some of the feature selection methods.

Information gain, the basic idea behind information gain is to find out how well each feature distinguishes the given data set. Information gain is frequently used to find out the term goodness in machine learning. Information gain of a term measures the number of bits of information obtained for category prediction by the presence or absence of the term in a document. If $\{C_i\}_{i=1}^m$ is the set of categories in a target space and m is the number of class

then information gain of a term t can be defined by the following equation:

$$IG(t) = -\sum_{i=1}^m p(C_i)\log p(C_i) +$$

$$p(t)\sum_{i=1}^m p(C_i \mid t)\log p(C_i \mid t) +$$

$$p(\bar{t})\sum_{i=1}^m p(C_i \mid \bar{t})\log p(C_i \mid \bar{t})$$

The first equation calculates the overall entropy of the training set, while the last two equations calculate the entropy of the feature, so we can simplistically represent the information gain of a feature by using the following formula:

IG (feature) = Entropy (training set) – Entropy (Feature)

After computing information gain for all features, we can use the features with the highest information gain score as features in any text categorization classifier.

Mutual information

In order to understand the association of words in a given corpus we can use a statistical model such as mutual information. In a two way contingency table where:

- x is a term
- y is a category
- A_x Number of times the x and y co-occur
- B_x Number of times the x occurs without y
- C_y Number of times the y occurs without x
- N Total number of documents

Then mutual information between *t* and *c* can be defined by:

$$I(x,y) = \log \frac{P_r(x \wedge y)}{P_r(x) * P_r(y)}$$

And is estimated using:

$$I(x,y) \approx \log \frac{A_x * N}{(A_x + C_y) * (A_x + B_x)}$$

The goodness of a term in global feature selection can be measured in two ways:

$$I_{avg}(x) = \sum_{i=1}^{m} P_r\left(C_{y_i}\right) I(x, C_{y_i})$$

$$I_{max}(x) = {}_{i=1}^{m} max \{I(x, C_y)\}$$

$$x^2$$

Statistic Chi Square feature selection

Another popular feature selection method is Chi Square. This method is used in statistics to measure the independence between the two variables, term t and class c. In feature selection we use this test to find out if the occurrence of a specific term and the occurrence of a specific class is independent; from this we can measure the quality of the terms. The null-hypothesis is that the two variables are completely independent of each other; the higher the value the $\chi2$ indicates, the closer relationship the variables have. If:

- *x* is a term
- *y* is a category
- A_x is the number of times the x and y co-occur
- B_x is the number of times the x occur without y
- C_y is the number of times the y occurs without x
- D_o is the number of times x and y does not occur
- *N* is the number of documents

The term goodness can be defined by:

$$X^2(t,c) = \frac{N*(A_x D_o - C_y B_x)^2}{(A_x + C_y)*(B_x + D_o)*(A_x + B_x)*(C_y + D_o)}$$

The x^2 statics for each term can be defined by:

$$X_{avg}^2(x) = \sum_{i=1}^{m} P_r(y_i) X^2(x, y_i)$$

$$X_{max}^2(x) = max_{i=1}^{m}\{X^2(x, y_i)\}$$

Frequency-based feature selection

In frequency-based feature selection, we first choose all the terms which are common in a category. Then we calculate the frequency of the terms; the frequency may be document frequency or collection frequency. Document frequency is well suited for the Bernoulli model and collection frequency is good when we are using a multinomial model. One main drawback of this technique is that the model may select some terms that are very frequent, but does not provide any information about the class. Though less accurate, this model works well if thousands of features are selected and is a good alternative to complex techniques such as **Inverse Document Frequency (IDF)**.

A commonly used measure of a term's selective potential is calculated by its inverse document frequency or IDF. The formula for IDF is calculated as follows:

$$idf(term) = log\frac{N}{df(term)}$$

Here, N is the number of documents in the corpus and *idf(term)* is the number of documents in which the term appears.

The weight of a term's appearance in a document is calculated by combining the term's frequency (or TF in the document) with its inverse document frequency or IDF:

$$w(t,d) = tfd(t)*idf(t)$$

This term–document score is known as TF*IDF, and is widely used.

Sentence completion

This is an interesting application of natural language processing. Sentence auto-completion is an interesting feature that is shockingly absent in our modern-day browsers and mobile interfaces. Getting grammatically and contextually relevant suggestions as to what to type next, while we are typing a few words, would be such a great feature to have.

Coursera, in one of the data science courses by Johns Hopkins, provided four compressed datasets that contain terms and frequencies of unigram, bigram, trigram, and 4-gram in four datasets. The problem at hand was to come up with a model that can learn to predict relevant words to type next.

The following code uses the Katz-Backoff algorithm, leveraging the four n-gram term frequency datasets to predict the next word in a sentence:

```
library(tm)
library(stringr)
# Load the n-gram data
load("/data_frame1.RData");
load("/data_frame2.RData");
load("/data_frame3.RData");
load("/data_frame4.RData");
CleanInputString<- function(input_string)
{
  # cleaning up data
input_string<- iconv(input_string, "latin1", "ASCII", sub=" ");
input_string<- gsub("[^[:alpha:][:space:][:punct:]]", "", input_
string);
  # corpus
input_corpus<- VCorpus(VectorSource(input_string))
input_corpus<- tm_map(input_corpus, content_transformer(tolower))
input_corpus<- tm_map(input_corpus, removePunctuation)
input_corpus<- tm_map(input_corpus, removeNumbers)
input_corpus<- tm_map(input_corpus, stripWhitespace)
input_string<- as.character(input_corpus[[1]])
input_string<- gsub("(^[[:space:]]+|[[:space:]]+$)", "", input_string)
if (nchar(input_string) > 0) {
return(input_string);
  } else {
return("");
  }
}
Get_next_word<- function(input_string)
{
```

```
    # Data cleansing using the function written earlier
input_string<- CleanInputString(input_string);
  # extract the string length
input_string<- unlist(strsplit(input_string, split=" "));
input_stringLen<- length(input_string);
next_word_present<- FALSE;
term_next<- as.character(NULL);
# Katz- backoffN-gram model
if (input_stringLen>= 3 & !next_word_present)
  {
    # collate the terms
    input_string1 <- paste(input_string[(input_stringLen-2):input_
stringLen], collapse=" ");
    # take the subset of 4-gram data
searchStr<- paste("^",input_string1, sep = "");
    data_frame4Temp <- data_frame4[grep (searchStr, data_
frame4$terms), ];
if ( length(data_frame4Temp[,1]) > 1 )
    {
term_next<- data_frame4Temp[1:10,1];# select 10 matching terms
next_word_present<- TRUE;
    }
    data_frame4Temp <- NULL;
  }
  # 2. lets go to n-1 gram
if (input_stringLen>= 2 & !next_word_present)
  {
    # collate input terms
    input_string1 <- paste(input_string[(input_stringLen-1):input_
stringLen], collapse=" ");
searchStr<- paste("^",input_string1, sep = "");
    data_frame3Temp <- data_frame3[grep (searchStr, data_
frame3$terms), ];
if ( length(data_frame3Temp[, 1]) > 1 )
    {
term_next<- data_frame3Temp[1:10,1];
next_word_present<- TRUE;
    }
    data_frame3Temp <- NULL;
  }
if (input_stringLen>= 1 & !next_word_present)
  {
    input_string1 <- input_string[input_stringLen];
searchStr<- paste("^",input_string1, sep = "");
```

```
        data_frame2Temp <- data_frame2[grep (searchStr, data_
frame2$terms), ];
if ( length(data_frame2Temp[, 1]) > 1 )
        {
term_next<- data_frame2Temp[1:10,1];
next_word_present<- TRUE;
        }
        data_frame2Temp <- NULL;
    }
if (!next_word_present&input_stringLen> 0)
    {
term_next<- data_frame1$terms[1,1];
    }
word_nxt<- word(term_next, -1);
if (input_stringLen> 0){
df<- data.frame(word_nxt);
return(df);
    } else {
word_nxt<- "";
df<- data.frame(word_nxt);
return(df);
    }
}
```

Let's try out the function for an incomplete sentence:

```
Get_next_word("I AM")
word_nxt
1          so
2           a
3         not
4       going
5          in
6        sure
7         the
8       still
9        just
10        now
Get_next_word("I AM SO")
word_nxt
1    excited
2      happy
3       glad
4   thankful
5      proud
```

```
 6    blessed
 7      tired
 8         so
 9    jealous
10       very
```

Summary

Topic modeling is an excellent method that has a wide range of applications in information retrieval from text data. In this chapter, we learned about a few topic modeling methods, and its implementation using R. We also learned about feature extraction and text clustering using R. Last, but not least, we took a practical real-world problem, to build a baseline sentence completing application.

In the next chapter, we are going to dive into supervised learning algorithms and their use in text classification.

6

Text Classification

Text classification is an extensively used phenomenon in natural language processing which has widespread utility in the different domains. Also known as text categorization, text classification finds its usage in various tasks related to information retrieval and management. Spam detection in e-mails, opinion mining or sentiment analysis on social media data, priority e-mail sorting, intent identification from user queries in chatbots, and automated query answering mechanisms are a few examples where text categorization has proved to be highly effective. In earlier chapters, we have discussed various feature selection and dimensionality reduction methods, which are preprocessing steps before text classification. We will briefly discuss supervised learning or classification mechanisms, how a learner is designed, and then we will move on to their implementation in terms of text data. We will also discuss the different cross-validation and evaluation mechanisms to evaluate the efficiency of the classification models, briefly discussing the diagnostic procedure on learners to yield better accuracy as well.

In this chapter, we will cover the following topics:

- Classification mechanism for text analysis
- Different classification techniques in text mining, with a detailed focus on linear and probabilistic classifiers:
    - ◦ Naive Bayes
    - ◦ Support vector machines
    - ◦ Maximum entropy
    - ◦ Decision trees
- Model evaluation
- Learning curve: bias-variance tradeoff

Text classification

The digital era has seen a humongous increase in data, which is unstructured and needs to be processed to extract any information out of it. Research in the field of natural language processing has paved the way towards automatic organization and classification of documents into the categories that they belong to. Document classification finds its utility in numerous applications such as spam classification, mail routing, priority inbox or mail relevance ranking, news monitoring and censoring, identification or article genre, and indexing of documents. The text classification process flow is described in the following diagram. We have discussed the preprocessing steps in *Chapter 5, Text Summarization and Clustering*, which involves basic data cleansing. After this step, we choose the document representation method. Features extraction and selection is performed on the cleansed data as per the document representation method chosen in the last step. We have discussed feature extraction, feature selection, and dimensionality reduction in *Chapter 5, Text Summarization and Clustering*. So, we will concentrate on the classification process throughout this chapter as shown in the following diagram:

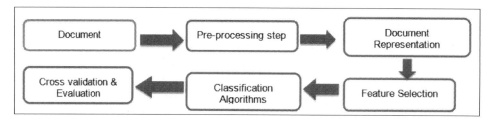

Document representation

The first step in the text classification process is to figure out how to represent the document in a manner which is suitable for classification tasks and learning algorithms. This step is basically intended to reduce the complexity of documents, making it easier to work with. While doing so, the following questions come to mind:

- Do we need to preserve the order of words?
- Is losing the information about the order a concern for us?

An attribute value representation of documents implies that the order of words in a document is not of high significance and each unique word in a document can be considered as a feature and the frequency of its occurrence is represented as a value. Further, discarding the features with a very low *value* or occurrence in the document can reduce the high dimensionality.

Vector space representation of words considers each word in a document as a vector. The attribute value representation may be having a Boolean form, set-of-words approach that captures the presence or absence of a word in a document, that is, if a particular word exists in a document or not. Apart from this representation, *tf*idf*, that is, term frequency multiplied by inverse document frequency, term weights can also be estimated and used as features.

Vector space models have some limitations too. For example, the document representation is very high dimensionally, and it may also lead to the loss of semantic relations or correlations between the different terms in the given documents. Analyzing text documents is tedious because there exists a near independence among the features; vocabulary size is huge, sometimes even larger than the number of instances. There will be certain words that occur a number of times, while there are words which will occur just a few times. How do we assign weights to the common words compared to rare words? Thus, document representation becomes an important part of this process.

Vector space models work on the ideology that we can derive the theme or meaning of a document based on the terms that constitute the document. If we represent each document as a vector, each unique term in the document acts like a dimension in the space.

Feature hashing

Feature hashing is a very efficient way to store data and reduce memory footprints. It requires less preprocessing, and it is a very effective way of dealing with large datasets. The Document Term Matrix holds all the data in the memory. When we apply a sparse function to this matrix, it will only retain all the data that are non-zero values. If the Document Term Matrix has lot of zeroes, we can use this and create a sparse matrix and reduce the memory footprint, but the sparse matrix function scans the entire data space to know which are the non-zero elements that it has to hold. Feature hashing is more efficient as it does not need a full scan; by holding the references or hashes addressed it can do the preprocessing at runtime or on the fly. When we are dealing with text data, very large matrices of features are formed. In order to reduce this to more relevant ones we remove the sparse terms, or take the top popular terms and discard the rest. In these types of solutions, we lose data, but in feature hashing, we don't lose any data.

Feature hashing is very useful tool when the user does not know the dimension of the feature vector. When we are performing text analysis, most of the time we consider the document as a bag-of-word representation and don't give much importance to the sequence in which the word appears. In this kind of document classification problem, we have to scan the entire dataset to know how many words we have, and find the dimension of the feature vector. In general, feature hashing is useful when we are working on streaming data or distributed data because it is difficult to know the real dimension of the feature vector.

The hash size tells us how big the data space should be, that is, the number of columns in the Document Term Matrix. We need to keep in mind the memory requirements and speed of the algorithm execution while selecting the hash size. We may choose this value empirically through trial and error. If it is too small, it may cause collisions (feature space collision), if it is too big the processing may become slow. There are text classification models which perform well with feature hashing.

`glmnet` and `xgboost` are a few of the R packages that support it.

Datasets supported by feature hashing include:

- Characters and factors
- Numerics and integers
- Arrays

Wush Wu Feature Hashing developed the package available on CRAN. The following is the definition from the documentation:

> *"Feature hashing, also called the hashing trick, is a method to transform features to vector. Without looking up the indices in an associative array, it applies a hash function to the features and uses their hash values as indices directly. The method of feature hashing in this package was proposed in Weinberger et. al. (2009). The hashing algorithm is the murmurhash3 from the digest package. Please see the README.md for more information."*

Classifiers – inductive learning

Classification or the supervised learning mechanism in machine learning, is the process of learning concepts or patterns generalizing the relationship between the dependent and independent variables, given a labeled or annotated data. A typical text classification task can be defined as follows:

- **Task T**: to classify opinions (positive or negative)
- **Performance measure P**: percentage of opinions correctly classified

- **Training experience E**: Annotated or labeled data to train the model on

Let's say, we have an opinion classification problem at hand. The training data contains texts as instances and opinions (positive or negative) as the outcome variable. The objective is to design a learning mechanism to be able to utilize the patterns in the training data to predict/label the outcome variable in an unknown or test dataset.

In order to learn the target concept or pattern, each instance *t* along with the associated concept *c(t)* from the training set is presented to the learner. The task assigned to the learning mechanism is to estimate the function *c*, such that the target concept stays generalized over most of the training instances and can be applied on unknown instances with high precision. The classifier creates a hypothesis for every training instance presented to it in conjunction with the associated label for the given instance. Once all the instances are observed, we have a large set of hypotheses generated, which are very specific in nature. With the inductive learning hypothesis principle, we know that, if a hypothesis can effectively approximate the target concept over a sufficiently large number of instances, it will also effectively approximate over an unknown set of instances. Such a hypothesis needs to be a generalized one as the specific hypothesis can approximate over a sufficiently large of number of instances and it would prove to be insufficient to approximate over unobserved instances.

Let's take a simple example to explain the concept of generalized and specific hypotheses. Suppose we have some data, corresponding to information about rain on a given day. The attributes given to us are temperature, humidity, and wind speed.

Let's consider two hypotheses trying to approximate the target concept of learning about the possibility of rain on a given day:

- Temperature = 30 degrees, humidity = 49%, wind speed = 8km/hr: it will not rain

- Temperature = 30 degrees, humidity= 49%, wind speed=? (can take any value): it will not rain.

The first hypothesis is very specific in nature and it is highly unlikely that it can be approximated over more than just a few instances, while the second hypothesis is comparatively less specific and more generalized than the first one and it is more likely to fit on a larger number of instances.

Once all the possible hypotheses are generated, the learning mechanism sorts them in general-to-specific ordering. As we have discussed, it is desired to have more generalized hypotheses than specific ones. Given the large number of hypotheses generated, how do we go about choosing the optimal hypotheses?

There are a few methods recommended for this issue (*Tom M. Mitchell*, 1997). The Candidate Elimination, Find-S, and List-Then-Eliminate algorithms are used to eliminate the redundant and highly specific hypotheses to learn a generalized hypothesis . The details of these algorithms are not in the scope of this book. The basic ideology behind these algorithms is to search for hypotheses in the version space, which is a subset of the set created with all the possible hypotheses from the training data; and compare them to the other training instances to see how well they can generalize over multiple instances. Subsequently, they keep eliminating the redundant hypotheses or keep merging specific ones to give a more generalized structure.

Tree-based learning

In machine learning, the decision tree is a well-known classification algorithm. In this type of classifying methodology, we create a decision tree model. When we provide an input for a prediction based on the input variable it traverses through the nodes and reaches the leaf node which is nothing but the classifier class. When the target variables have a finite set of values it is called a classification tree, which we will discuss in this section. If the target variables take continuous values it is called regression trees.

Let us understand some basic terminologies used in the decision tree. The decision tree is constructed based on input variables. The number of input variables will alter the classification output; in technical terms, these input variables are also called attributes. In text mining, if we are classifying a set of documents into different topics, the significant words in the document become the attributes and the topics which are the resulting outcome become the classes.

The following is a simple diagram of a decision tree:

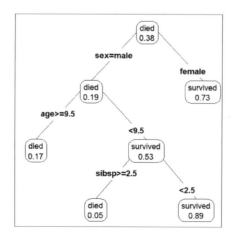

The tree is made up of branches and nodes. Every branch from a node signifies the outcome using one of the attributes. The nodes that do not have any branches are called leaf nodes. These nodes are at the end of the tree, and they are the final classes of the classification problem. Decision trees are built by recursively splitting training data so that each division tends towards one class. Every node that is not a leaf node has a branch and each branch is the outcome of one or more attributes which further influences how the data will be divided further. The split is made in such a way such that the data is distinct or as distinct as possible. In ML terms, this is called a pure leaf node; each division is either pure or we can improve the performance by increasing the generalization by pruning the tree.

Partitioning of data for splitting the node depends on the attributes used to split it. In order to construct the tree, we need to select the best splitting attribute. There are various algorithms used to build a decision tree. At a high level, these algorithms try to solve the challenges in their own optimal way as explained in the following steps:

1. Select the best attributes for splitting and determine the split values.
2. Ascertain the number of splits at each node.
3. Ascertain the order of the attribute that has to be considered for splitting. Can the attributes be considered only once or many times?
4. Choose the pruning method for the tree: pre pruning or post-pruning.
5. Choose the growth and stopping criteria for the tree.

In order to perform an optimal split and evaluate the goodness of the split, there are various methods:

- Gini index
- Information gain
- Entropy
- Split info
- Gain ratio

Some of the well-known algorithms used in building decision trees are:

- ID3
- C4.5
- C5
- CART
- CHAID
- SPRINT

There are various pros and cons of decision trees. The pros are:

- They are easy to understand and visualize. The interpretability makes them a good choice in scenarios where simplicity of the model is preferred over accuracy.

- They can be used in case of both categorical data and numerical data.

- The performance of the model can be assessed using various statistical methods. Huge datasets can be analyzed in a reasonable amount of time since the algorithms are less complex and easy to compute.

- Decision trees perform feature selections implicitly.

- Non-linear relationships between variables do not cause issues in performance.

Some cons are that the decision trees generated may become very complex and do not generalize well. However, pruning techniques can be applied to resolve this.

In the following code, we are detecting if the speech is given by Obama or Romney based on the input document. We will use the rpart library to build the decision tree:

rpart code for decision trees:

```
library(tm)
library(rpart)
```

1. Load the files into the corpus:

```
obamaCorpus <- Corpus(DirSource(directory = "D:/R/Chap 6/Speeches/
obama" , encoding="UTF-8"))

romneyCorpus <- Corpus(DirSource(directory = "D:/R/Chap 6/
Speeches/romney" , encoding="UTF-8"))
```

2. Merge both the corpus to one big corpus:

```
fullCorpus <- c(obamaCorpus,romneyCorpus)#1-22 (obama),
23-44(romney)
```

3. Do basic processing on the loaded corpus.

4. Now we will perform basic cleansing on the data. That includes removing punctuation marks, stripping whitespaces, converting the text to lower case, and removing stop words from the text data:

```
fullCorpus.cleansed <- tm_map(fullCorpus, removePunctuation)
```

```
fullCorpus.cleansed <- tm_map(fullCorpus.cleansed,
stripWhitespace)

fullCorpus.cleansed <- tm_map(fullCorpus.cleansed, tolower)

fullCorpus.cleansed <- tm_map(fullCorpus.cleansed, removeWords,
stopwords("english"))

fullCorpus.cleansed <- tm_map(fullCorpus.cleansed,
PlainTextDocument)
```

5. **Create the Document Term Matrix for analysis:**

```
full.dtm <- DocumentTermMatrix(fullCorpus.cleansed)
```

6. **Remove the sparse terms:**

```
full.dtm.spars <- removeSparseTerms(full.dtm , 0.6)
```

7. **Convert the DocumentTermMatrix to a data frame for easy manipulation:**

```
full.matix <- data.matrix(full.dtm.spars)
full.df <- as.data.frame(full.matix)
```

8. **Add the speaker's name to the data frame:**

```
full.df[,"SpeakerName"] <- "obama"
full.df$SpeakerName[21:44] <- "romney"
```

9. **Create the Training and Test Index:**

```
train.idx <- sample(nrow(full.df) , ceiling(nrow(full.df)* 0.6))
test.idx <- (1:nrow(full.df))[-train.idx]
```

10. **Select the top 70 terms used in the corpus:**

```
freqterms70 <- findFreqTerms( full.dtm.spars, 70)
```

11. **Create the formulas for input to the rpart function:**

```
outcome <- "SpeakerName"
formula_str <- paste(outcome, paste(freqterms70, collapse=" + "),
sep=" ~ ")
```

```
formula <- as.formula(formula_str)

fit <- rpart(formula, method="class", data=full.
df.train,control=rpart.control(minsplit=5, cp=0.001));

print(fit)
```

12. Display the cp table The output is as follows:

    ```
    n= 27


    1) root 27 13 romney (0.4814815 0.5185185)
      2) health>=2.5 8   0 obama (1.0000000 0.0000000) *
      3) health< 2.5 19   5 romney (0.2631579 0.7368421)
        6) america< 3 3   0 obama (1.0000000 0.0000000) *
        7) america>=3 16   2 romney (0.1250000 0.8750000)
          14) one>=10 2   0 obama (1.0000000 0.0000000) *
          15) one< 10 14   0 romney (0.0000000 1.0000000) *


    printcp(fit)
    ```

13. Plot the cross-validation results.

14. Classification tree:

    ```
    rpart(formula = formula, data = full.df.train, method = "class",
        control = rpart.control(minsplit = 5, cp = 0.001))
    ```

15. The output is as follows:

    ```
    Variables actually used in tree construction:
    [1] Care

    Root node error: 13/27 = 0.48148

    n= 27
    ```

	CP	nsplit	rel error	xerror	xstd
1	0.61538	0	1.00000	1.53846	0.17516
2	0.23077	1	0.38462	0.53846	0.17516
3	0.15385	2	0.15385	0.76923	0.19302
4	0.00100	3	0.00000	0.69231	0.18842

16. Let's plot the tree:

```
par(mfrow = c(1,2), xpd = NA)
text(fit, use.n=T)
```

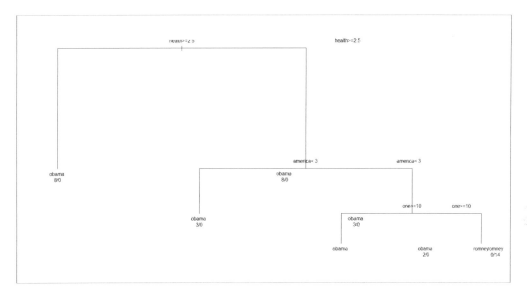

The preceding image depicts the decision tree just created. At each node based on the attribute in the sentence it provides a weight to detect if it's an Obama speech or Romney speech.

Bayesian classifiers: Naive Bayes classification

Naive Bayes classifiers are probabilistic classifiers, built using the Bayes theorem, Naive Bayes is also known as priori probability and a class conditional probability classifier, since it uses prior probability of each feature and generates a posterior probability distribution over all the features.

This classifier makes the following assumptions about the data:

- It assumes all the features in the dataset are independent of each other
- It assumes all the features are important

Though these assumptions may not be true in real world scenario, Naive Bayes is still used in many applications for text classification, such as:

- Spam filtering for e-mail applications
- Social media mining, such as finding the sentiments in a given text
- Computer network security applications

This is because the classifier has its own strengths, such as:

- Naive Bayes classifiers are highly scalable and need less computational cycles when compared with other advanced and sophisticated classifiers
- A huge number of features can be taken into consideration
- They work well even when there is missing data and the dimensionality of the inputs is high
- They need only small amounts of training sets

Let's do a hands-on exercise on the Naive Bayes classifier.

E-mail is a one of the most widely used applications for communication. The following is an screenshot of an inbox:

Our inbox is cluttered with lot of e-mails every day; some of them are important, others are promotional e-mails, phishing e-mails, spam e-mails, and so on.

Let's build a spam classifier that can reduce the clutter by segregating the spam from the real important ones:

1. We will set up the environment by loading all the required library.
2. The dataset used in this code can be downloaded from `http://www.aueb.gr/users/ion/data/enron-spam/`
3. The data is Enron-Spam in pre-processed form: Enron1

```
install.packages("caret")
require(caret)
```

```
install.packages("kernlab")
require(kernlab)

install.packages("e1071")
require(e1071)

install.packages("tm")
require(tm)

install.packages("plyr")
require(plyr)
```

4. Extract the Enron-Spam dataset to your local filesystem. In my case it's in the following directory:

```
pathName <- "D:/R/Chap 6/enron1"
```

5. The dataset has two sub-folders: the spam folder contains all the mails that are spam ,and the ham folder contains all the mails that are legitimate:

```
emailSubDir <- c("ham","spam")
```

Let's write a function that can build the Term Document Matrix from the text input.

1. Build a Term Document Matrix. Here we are converting the text to a quantitative format for analysis:

```
GenerateTDMForEMailCorpus <- function(subDir , path){
```

2. Concatenate the variable, that is, the path and the sub-folder name to create the complete path to the mail corpus directory:

```
#mailDir <- sprintf("%s/%s", path, subDir)

mailDir <-paste(path, subDir, sep="/")
```

3. Create a corpus using the preceding computed directory path. We will use `DirSource` since we are dealing with directories, with encoding UTF-8:

```
mailCorpus <- Corpus(DirSource(directory = mailDir ,
encoding="UTF-8"))
```

4. Create the Term Document Matrix:

```
mail.tdm <- TermDocumentMatrix(mailCorpus)
```

5. Remove sparse terms from TDM for better analysis:

```
mail.tdm <- removeSparseTerms(mail.tdm,0.7)
```

```
Return the results: the list of TDM for spam and ham:
```

```
result <- list(name = subDir , tdm = mail.tdm)
```

```
}
```

Let's write a function that can convert the Term Document Matrix to a data frame.

1. We will convert the TDM to a data frame and append the type of mail if it's a spam or ham in the data frame:

```
BindMailTypeToTDM <- function(individualTDM){
```

2. Create a numeric matrix, get its transpose so that the column contains the words and the row contains the number of word occurrences in the mail:

```
mailMatrix <- t(data.matrix(individualTDM[["tdm"]]))
```

3. Convert this matrix into a data frame since it's easy to work with data frames:

```
mailDataFrame <- as.data.frame(mailMatrix , stringASFactors =
FALSE)
```

4. Add the type of mail to each row in the data frame:

```
mailDataFrame <- cbind(mailDataFrame , rep(individualTDM[["name"]]
, nrow(mailDataFrame)))
```

5. Give a proper name to the last column of the data frame:

```
colnames(mailDataFrame)[ncol(mailDataFrame)] <- "MailType"
return (mailDataFrame)


}


tdmList <- lapply(emailSubDir , GenerateTDMForEMailCorpus , path =
pathName)


mailDataFrame <- lapply(tdmList, BindMailTypeToTDM)
```

6. Join both the data frames for spam and ham:

```
allMailDataFrame <- do.call(rbind.fill , mailDataFrame)
```

7. Fill the empty columns with 0:

```
allMailDataFrame[is.na(allMailDataFrame)] <- 0
```

8. Reorder the column for readability:

```
allMailDataFrame_ordered <- allMailDataFrame[ ,c(1:18,20:23,19)]
```

9. Prepare a training set. We are getting about 60% of the rows to train the model:

```
train.idx <- sample(nrow(allMailDataFrame_ordered) ,
ceiling(nrow(allMailDataFrame_ordered)* 0.6))
```

10. Prepare the test set, with the remaining rows that are not part of training sample:

```
test.idx <- (1:nrow(allMailDataFrame_ordered))[-train.idx]


allMailDataFrame.train <- allMailDataFrame_ordered[train.idx,]


allMailDataFrame.test <- allMailDataFrame_ordered[test.idx,]


trainedModel <- naiveBayes(allMailDataFrame.train[,c(1:22)],allMai
lDataFrame.train[,c(23)], data = allMailDataFrame.train)


prediction <- predict(trainedModel, allMailDataFrame.test)


confusionMatrix <- confusionMatrix(prediction,allMailDataFrame.
test[,c(23)])


confusionMatrix
```

11. Confusion Matrix and Statistics

```
              Reference
Prediction ham spam
      ham   855    1
      spam 626   586


            Accuracy : 0.6968
              95% CI : (0.6765, 0.7166)
 No Information Rate : 0.7162
 P-Value [Acc > NIR] : 0.9753
```

```
ctable <- as.table(matrix(c(634    , 1, 466 , 450), nrow = 2, byrow
= TRUE))
```

```
fourfoldplot(ctable, color = c("#CC6666", "#99CC99"), conf.level =
0, margin = 1, main = "Confusion Matrix")
```

Here is the depiction of the Confusion Matrix:

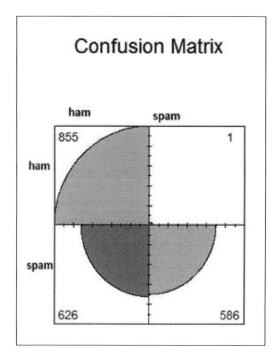

K-Nearest neighbors

The **K-Nearest neighbors** algorithm (**k-NN**) works on the principle of distance functions for a given pair of points. It is very easy to implement and non-parametric algorithm in nature. In K-Nearest neighbor classifier, k is an integer greater than zero. This is a simple classification technique used to find the k, nearest data points in a dataset to a given data point. The biggest challenge with this classifier is to find out the optimal value for k which depends on the data. k-NN uses all the features for computing the distance and because of this the complexity for searching the nearest neighbors increases, which is one of the major drawbacks, since all the attributes or features in the dataset may not be very significant. Thus, providing certain weights to them based on significance, may increase the classifier accuracy.

The error rate of the k-NN classifier, P_{k-nn} can be equated to:

$$\lim_{\substack{N,k \to \infty \\ \frac{k}{N} \to 0,}} P_{k-nn} = P_B$$

- N : is the set of points
- k: is the set of classes
- P_B is the Bayes error rate

In the case where $k=1$, it is called the nearest neighbor classifier. The error rate for this can be calculated using the following equation:

$$P_{1-nn} \leq 2P_B$$

Let $x = (x1, x2, ..., xn)$ be the predicted points, then given a point $a = (a1, a2, ..., an)$, we identify k observations in the training dataset that are similar to a. Neighbors are defined by a distance that we calculate between observations based on the independent variables. There are various ways where we can calculate the distance between the points: one of them is the **Euclidean distance**.

The Euclidean distance between the points $(x1, x2, ..., xn)$ and $(a1, a2, ..., an)$ is defined as:

$$\sqrt{(x_1 - a_1)^2 + (x_2 - a_2)^2 + \cdots + (x_n - a_n)^2}$$

For each n-dimensional object, the Euclidean distances between the specified object and all the training data objects are calculated and the specified object is assigned the class label that most of the *k* closest training data has. The curse of dimensionality and large feature sets are a problem for k-nn.

Let us classify the speeches of US presidential candidates using k-nn:

1. Load library using the following code:

    ```
    install.packages("class")
    require(class)

    install.packages("tm")
    require(tm)

    install.packages("plyr")
    require(plyr)

    install.packages("caret")
    require(caret)
    ```

2. To make sure strings are not converted to nominal or categorical variables, we set the following option:

    ```
    options(stringAsFactors = FALSE)
    ```

3. Extract the Speech dataset to your local filesystem. In my case it's in the following directory:

    ```
    speechDir <- c("romney","obama")
    ```

4. The dataset has two sub-folders: the obama folder contains all the speeches from Obama ,and the romney folder contains all the speeches that are from Romney:

    ```
    pathToSpeeches <- "D:/R/Chap 6/Speeches"
    ```

5. Data cleaning is an essential step when we do analysis on text data, such as removing numbers, stripping whitespaces, removing punctuation, removing stop words, and, changing to lowercase:

    ```
    CleanSpeechText <- function(speechText){
    ```

6. We will remove all punctuation characters from the text:

    ```
    speechText.cleansed <- tm_map(speechText, removePunctuation)
    ```

7. We will remove all whitespace from the text:

    ```
    speechText.cleansed <- tm_map(speechText, stripWhitespace)
    ```

8. We will convert all the words to lowercase:

```
speechText.cleansed <- tm_map(speechText, tolower)
```

9. We will remove all stop words related to English:

```
speechText.cleansed <- tm_map(speechText, removeWords,
stopwords("english"))
```

10. Return the cleansed text:

```
return (speechText.cleansed)
}
```

11. We will build a term document matrix. Here we are converting the text to quantitative format for analysis:

```
produceTDM <- function(speechFolder,path){
```

12. Concatenate the strings to get the full path to the respective speeches:

```
speechDirPath <-paste(path, speechFolder, sep="/")
```

13. Since it's a directory use `DirSource` to create the corpus:

```
speechCorpus <- Corpus(DirSource(directory = speechDirPath ,
encoding="UTF-8"))
```

14. Clean this corpus to remove unwanted noise in the text to make our analysis better:

```
speechCorpus.cleansed <- CleanSpeechText(speechCorpus)
```

15. Build the term document matrix for this cleansed corpus:

```
speech.tdm <- TermDocumentMatrix(speechCorpus.cleansed)
```

16. Remove the sparse terms to improve the prediction:

```
speech.tdm <- removeSparseTerms(speech.tdm,0.6)
```

17. Returns the result of both the speeches as a list of tdm:

```
resultTdmList <- list(name = speechFolder , tdm = speech.tdm)
}
```

18. We will add the speaker's name to the TDM for training and testing:

```
addSpeakerName <- function(individualTDM){
```

19. Create a numeric matrix, get its transpose so that the column contains the words and the row contains the number of word occurrences in the speech:

```
speech.matix <- t(data.matrix(individualTDM[["tdm"]]))
```

20. Convert this matrix into data frame since it's easy to work with data frames:

```
seech.df <- as.data.frame(speech.matix)
```

21. Add the speaker's name to each row in the data frame:

```
seech.df <- cbind(seech.df , rep(individualTDM[["name"]] ,
nrow(seech.df)))
```

22. Give a proper name to the last column of the data frame:

```
colnames(seech.df)[ncol(seech.df)] <- "SpeakerName"

return (seech.df)

}
```

```
tdmList <- lapply(speechDir , produceTDM , path = pathToSpeeches)
speechDfList <- lapply(tdmList, addSpeakerName)
```

23. Join both the data frames for Obama and Romney:

```
combinedSpeechDf <- do.call(rbind.fill , speechDfList)
```

24. Fill the empty columns with 0:

```
combinedSpeechDf[is.na(combinedSpeechDf)] <- 0
```

25. Prepare a training set. We are getting about 60% of the rows to train the modal:

```
train.idx <- sample(nrow(combinedSpeechDf) ,
ceiling(nrow(combinedSpeechDf)* 0.6))
```

26. Prepare the test set with the remaining rows that are not part of training sample:

```
test.idx <- (1:nrow(combinedSpeechDf))[-train.idx]
```

27. Let's create a data frame that only has the speaker names of the training set:

```
combinedSpeechDf.speakers <- combinedSpeechDf[,"SpeakerName"]
```

28. Let's create a data frame that contains all the attributes except the speaker name:

```
combinedSpeechDf.allAttr <- combinedSpeechDf[,!colnames(combinedSp
eechDf) %in% "SpeakerName"]
```

29. Let's use the preceding training set and test set to create inputs to our classifier:

```
combinedSpeechDf.train <- combinedSpeechDf.allAttr[train.idx,]
```

```
combinedSpeechDf.test <- combinedSpeechDf.allAttr[test.idx,]
```

```
combinedSpeechDf.trainOutcome <- combinedSpeechDf.speakers[train.idx]
```

```
combinedSpeechDf.testOutcome <- combinedSpeechDf.speakers[test.idx]
```

```
prediction <- knn(combinedSpeechDf.train ,combinedSpeechDf.test ,combinedSpeechDf.trainOutcome)
```

30. Let's check out the Confusion matrix:

```
confusionMatrix <- confusionMatrix(prediction,testOutcome)

Confusion Matrix and Statistics
          Reference
Prediction romney obama
    romney      5     0
    obama       4     8

          Accuracy : 0.7647
            95% CI : (0.501, 0.9319)
No Information Rate : 0.5294
```

Kernel methods

Kernel methods exploit the similarity between documents, that is, by length, topic, language, and so on, to extract patterns from the documents. Inner products between data items can reveal a lot of latent information; in fact many of the standard algorithms can be represented in the form of inner products between data items in a potentially complex feature space. The reason why kernel methods are suitable for high dimensional data is that the complexity only depends on the choice of kernel, it does not depend upon the features of the data in use. Kernels solve the computational issues by transforming the data into richer feature spaces and non-linear features and then applying linear classifier to the transformed data, as shown in the following diagram:

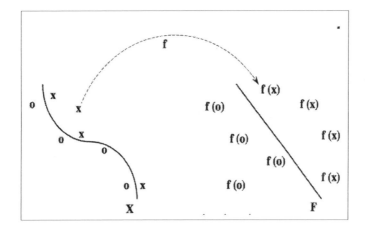

Some of the kernel methods available are:

- Linear kernel
- Polynomial kernel
- Radical base function kernel
- Sigmoid kernel

Support vector machines

Support vector machines (SVM) is a kernel method of classification, which gained a lot of traction among the classification mechanisms because of its ability to work well on high dimensional data. Unlike other classifiers, the complexity does not depend on the number of features, but the margin with it separates the instances into different classes. Thus, an increase in the number of dimensions does not affect the computational cost.

SVM is a non-probabilistic classifier, which in its basic configuration, is expected to learn a linear threshold function. But it can also be made to learn RBF networks, such as radial basis functions, polynomial functions, sigmoid neural nets, and so on.

SVM attempts to find a linear hyper plane, which can separate the data. It is also called a large margined classifier since it tries to find the hyper plane with the largest margin. Any linear learner has to estimate an explicit mapping in order to learn a non-linear function or work on a dataset with a non-linear decision boundary, as shown in the following diagram:

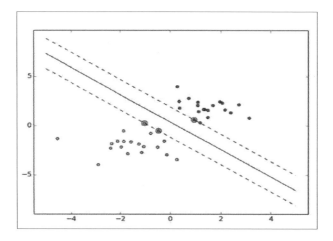

How do we choose the plane which is the best linear separator? If we join the points on both sides of the plane or the points owing to both the classes separately such that we get the most compact convex hull on both the sides. Once we get the convex hulls on both the sides, we draw a line joining the closest instance with the minimum margin between classes. The perpendicular bisector to this line is the optimal hyper plane which is the best linear separator. How do we find the closest points in the two convex hulls? This is done using an optimization algorithm as shown in the following diagram:

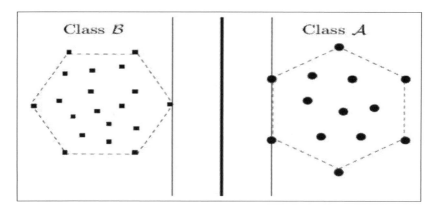

If A and B were two convex hulls created, suppose the line parallel to the convex hull A is $x'w=K$ and the line parallel to convex hull B is $x'w = n$, then the linear separator would be $x'w= k+n/2$.

The optimization problem to find the closest point in both the convex hulls is given by the following equation:

$$\min_{u,v} \quad \tfrac{1}{2}\left\|A'u - B'v\right\|^2$$
$$s.t. \quad e'u = 1 \quad e'v = 1 \quad u \geq 0 \quad v \geq 0$$

If $c = A'u$ and $d = B'v$ are the two convex hulls

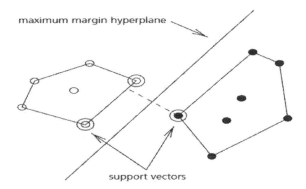

$$\hat{y} = \text{sgn} \sum_{i=1}^{n} w_i y_i k(\mathbf{x}_i, \mathbf{x}')$$

Where:

$\hat{y} \in \{-1, +1\}$ is the predicted label for the unseen input X'.

$k : \chi \times \chi \to \mathbb{R}$ is the kernel function that estimates the similarity between the input

data points and $w_i \in \mathbb{R}$ are the weights the sign function determines the predicted outcome to be negative or positive.

Kernel Trick

If we look at the following diagram, we can clearly see that the data in the first figure is not linearly separable. But if we map this data to a three-dimensional space, we observe that we can linearly separate the data now, using a hyperplane as the decision boundary. Transforming the instance space to a new non-linear mapping, Support vector machines are able to implement non-linear class boundaries. This phenomenon is called the **Kernel Trick.** A representation follows:

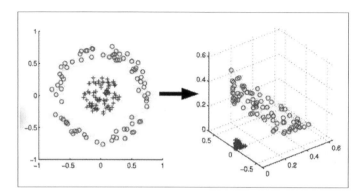

The Kernel Trick helps in using the dot product based methods in a possibly infinite dimensional feature space, without actually performing the computationally expensive process of projecting the features into such a high dimensional space explicitly:

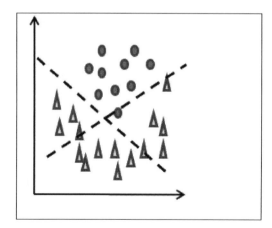

The preceding graph is for when the linear function cannot draw the hyperplane:

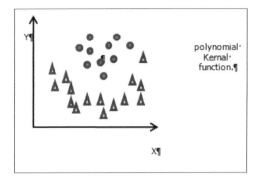

We can find out the best kernel function for our domain by running the classifiers through all the functions and analyzing the results. In the last two sections, we have shown you the basic steps of creating the DTM from text files. We will now use the speech TDM to run our SVN classifier and predict who gave that speech:

```
sv <- svm(combinedSpeechDf.train, combinedSpeechDf.trainOutcome)
pred <-predict(sv,combinedSpeechDf.test)
table(pred, combinedSpeechDf.testOutcome)
```

```
  pred       romney obama
  romney       10      0
  obama         0      7
```

R has a package `kernlab` that supports various kernel methods that can be applied to SVM.

`kernlab` provides implementations to the most used kernel functions such as:

- `rbfdot`: Radial Basis kernel "Gaussian"
- `polydot`: Polynomial kernel
- `vanilladot`: Linear kernel
- `tanhdot`: Hyperbolic tangent kernel
- `laplacedot`: Laplacian kernel
- `besseldot`: Bessel kernel
- `anovadot`: ANOVA RBF kernel
- `splinedot`: Spline kernel
- `stringdot`: String kernel

For more details go visit the `kernlab` at http://www.inside-r.org/node/63499

The `kernlab` package in R provides different kernels to be used, while the user can write their own kernel functions as well.

There are four basic kernel functions:

- **Linear**: $K(xi,xj) = xTi\ xj$.
- **Polynomial**: $K(xi,xj)=(\gamma xiTxj +r)d, \gamma>0$.
- **Radial Basis function (RBF)**: $K(xi,xj)=exp(-\gamma xi-xj2), \gamma>0$.
- **Sigmoid**: $K(xi,xj)=tanh(\gamma xiTxj +r)$.

Here, γ, r, and d are kernel parameters.

How to apply SVM on a real world example?

- Perform a data transformation appropriate to apply as per the SVM package:
  - Convert categorical variables into numeric data by using binary dummies.
  - For example, if there is a variable `gender`, there are two possible values for this categorical attribute. We can create binary dummies, `gender_male` and `gender_female`, as two variables replacing the variable gender. Thus each of the instances where the gender was male, in place of that we will have `gender_male` as 1 and `gender_female` as 0.

- Scale the data appropriately:
  - It is important to scale or normalize the data before applying SVM to counter any computational challenges.
  - Also, it may lead to issues if there is huge variance in the data.

- Select the kernel function.

  You can randomly select a kernel function and estimate the best parameters for the chosen kernel. Test the performance and further tune or select a different kernel function.

Normally, the Radial Basis function RBF is the first choice of kernel. It performs reasonably well when the decision boundary is non-linear, as it can effectively map the samples into the high dimensional space, which linear classifier cannot do.

Also, the number of hyper parameters that we need to optimize in order to get the best set of parameters to apply in case of RBF is lesser than the other polynomial kernel functions. In RBF, we need to choose a penalty parameter, $C(>0)$ and

It is also important to note that, when the dimensions are very high compared to the number of instances available to train on, the linear kernel would work better than RBF.

When to apply a linear kernel?

When the number of dimensions is significantly larger than the number of instances: In such a case, an explicit mapping to high dimensional space does not add any value. Thus even a linear kernel performs better.

When the dimensions as well as instances are large in number.

Number of instances is significantly larger than the number of dimensions.Maximum entropy classifier

Maximum entropy classifiers belong to an exponential class of models. These classify the instances based on the least biased estimate available from the given information or the constraints applicable. For example, let's consider a three-way classification task, where the prior information given is that on average 50% of the documents which contain the word equity belongs to the class investment. Based on this information, whichever document we find the word equity in, we assume there is a 50% probability of this document being classified as an investment class. What about the documents where we do not find the word equity? In such a case, we would assume a uniform class distribution, 33.33% each. Such a model, which complies with the constraints, is known as the maximum entropy model. Maximum entropy models provide us with the least biased estimate, complying with the constraints on conditional distribution, and are heavily noncommittal towards the missing information.

In the simplest terms, when we use statistical models to categorize instances associated to an unknown event, we should always categorize them based on the entropy estimates being the maximum. The principle of maximum entropy implies that given all the models that can fit to our training set, the model, which has the maximum entropy, should be chosen. The core ideology is to learn the probability distribution from the given dataset without assuming any prior distribution other than the observed one, and select the distribution with the maximum entropy subject to the constraints implied. Maximum entropy implies the least assumption and uniformity in distribution. Maxent models are different from the Naïve Bayes classifiers in their basic assumption over the feature independence. Naïve Bayes assumes the features to be conditionally independent to each other, while Maxent does not assume the same. Getting rid of this assumption makes Maxent classifiers, which are to be used regularly in the scenarios where either there is not much information on the prior probability distribution available or it is perceived to be unsafe, to assume the conditional independence of the attributes.

The objective is to utilize the context predicates or the information such as unigram, bigram, and other text characteristics, to build a stochastic model to assign a class to each of the context or instances. Assume the training data $T = \{(t1, c1), (t2, c2)...$ $(tN, cN)\}$ where $t1,t2,t3....$ are the context information and ci is the class assigned to the respective contexts. The training data is a set of context predicates, each of them represented by a vector or words. We would like to estimate a probability distribution that represents the contexts. Each context must be assigned to one of the classes $P(c1) + P(c2) + P(c3) + ...+ P(cN) = 1$.

As discussed at the onset of this section, if there is no prior information provided we assume a uniform distribution of the one with the least assumptions possible $P(c1) = P(c2) = P(c3) = ...= P(cN) = 1/N$.

Let's add some prior information to the scenario and observe how the distribution changes accordingly. Let's say, if there is prior information given to us that, if there is a word equity present in the contexts, there is a 50% probability of the context being classified as $c1$. How does this information affect the distribution we just came up with?

$P(c1 \mid equity) = 0.50$

$P(c2 \mid equity) = P(c3 \mid equity) = ...= P(cN \mid equity) = (1-0.50)/N$

Maxent implemenation in R

The Maxent package provides a low-memory implementation of multinomial logistic regression or the maximum entropy model. This package leverages a C++ library to perform a memory-efficient implementation of the maximum entropy algorithm, which consumes lot of memory if the corpus is large. The parameter estimation process is streamlined and the reduced number of parameters helps minimize the memory consumption. **L-BFGS, OWLQN**, and stochastic gradient descent optimization are the different optimization techniques used for parameter estimation.

```
library(maxent)
data <- read.csv(system.file("data/USCongress.csv.gz",package =
"maxent"))
```

We will use the tm package to build the corpus from the data that we loaded. After which, we will convert it to TermDocumentMatrix or DocumentTermMatrix. We will use the as.compressed.matrix() function from maxent package to convert the term document matrix or document matrix into a compressed matrix format, matrix.csr.

```
library(tm)
corpus <- Corpus(VectorSource(data$text))
dtm <- TermDocumentMatrix(corpus,
                          control=list(weighting = weightTfIdf,
                                       language = "english",
                                       tolower = TRUE,
                                       stopwords = TRUE,
                                       removeNumbers = TRUE,
                                       removePunctuation = TRUE,
                                       stripWhitespace = TRUE))
# This step is important, because maxent does not support tdm or dtm
formats, we'll convert the term document matrix to a compressed matrix

matrix_sp <- as.compressed.matrix(dtm)
```

Now, we will train our maxent model on the training data, specifying the independent and dependent variable.

```
# Not to run
maxent(feature_matrix, code_vector, l1_regularizer = 0, l2_regularizer
= 0, use_sgd = FALSE, set_heldout = 0, verbose = FALSE)
```

If the training sample is huge, its best advised to set the `use_sgd` argument as TRUE, to be able to use stochastic gradient descent.

`l1_regularizer` and `l2_regularizer` are set to 0 by default. In the event of over fitting, `l1_regulartization`, `l2_regularization` and `set_holdout` parameters can be tuned to overcome over fitting.

The number of iterations for SGD is set at 30 by default, and the learning rate alpha is set at 0.85 by default. L1 and L2 regularization cannot be used together, thus `l1_regularizer` and `l2_regularizer` should not be set together.

Stochastic gradient descent does not support L2 regularization, thus if `use_sgd` is set to be TRUE, the `l2_regularization` parameter should be left as the default value of 0.

```
max_model <- maxent(matrix_sp[,1:2000],data$major[1:200
0],use_sgd = TRUE,
                    set_heldout = 200)
```

We can also save the model, to save ourselves from training again, and be able to directly load the saved model and use it for predictions:

```
save.model(max_model, "Model")
max_model <- load.model("Model")
```

We will use the trained model to predict on the test data:

```
results <- predict(max_model, matrix_sp[,2001:2400])
```

The Maxent package provides a function, `tune.maxent`, to tune the maxent model. The parameters that are altered are `l1_regularizer`, `l2_regularizer`, `use_sgd`, and `set_holdout`. `l1_regularizer` and `l2_regularizer` vary between 0 to 1 at a space of `0.2` each. `Set_holdout` is the number of samples held out for cross-validation. K-fold cross-validation is used to validate the model to avoid overfiting.

```
model_tune <- tune.maxent(matrix_sp[,1:5000],+
data$major[1:5000],nfold=3, showall=TRUE)
```

```
model_tune
      l1_regularizer l2_regularizer use the_sgd set_heldout   accuracy
pct_best_fit:
```

[1,]	0.0	0.0	0	0	0.7215367
0.9460567					
[2,]	0.2	0.0	0	0	0.7416078
0.9723734					
[3,]	0.4	0.0	0	0	0.7412365
0.9718866					
[4,]	0.6	0.0	0	0	0.7364983
0.9656740					
[5,]	0.8	0.0	0	0	0.7291518
0.9560415					
[6,]	1.0	0.0	0	0	0.7211886
0.9456004					
[7,]	0.0	0.0	0	742	0.7215367
0.9460567					
[8,]	0.0	0.2	0	0	0.7626780
1.0000000					
[9,]	0.0	0.4	0	0	0.7540851
0.9887333					
[10,]	0.0	0.6	0	0	0.7479785
0.9807265					
[11,]	0.0	0.8	0	0	0.7407543
0.9712542					
[12,]	0.0	1.0	0	0	0.7371181
0.9664866					
[13,]	0.0	0.0	1	0	0.7598019
0.9962289					
[14,]	0.2	0.0	1	0	0.7416078
0.9723734					
[15,]	0.4	0.0	1	0	0.7412365
0.9718866					
[16,]	0.6	0.0	1	0	0.7364983
0.9656740					
[17,]	0.8	0.0	1	0	0.7291518
0.9560415					
[18,]	1.0	0.0	1	0	0.7211886
0.9456004					

```
optimal_model <- maxent(matrix_sp[,1:2000],data$major[1:2000],l2_
regularizer= 0.2, use_sgd = FALSE)


results <- predict(optimal_model, matrix_sp[,2001:2400])
```

RTextTools: a text classification framework

Until now we have seen how to run individual classifiers to classify text data. There are various R packages that support numerous classification methods. In order to begin analyzing data with various classifiers, you can use a very powerful yet simple to use R package called RTextTools. This package provides support to most widely used classifiers, and it also provides a tuning mechanism to experiment with different settings of algorithms for expert users. RTextTools uses a variety of existing R packages to support text pre-processing and machine learning algorithms.

The following are the basic steps to run various classifiers using RTextTools:

1. Load the data files. They can be csv, excel, and so on.

2. Create a matrix object. This is an object of the class, DocumentTermMatrix. We use the create_matrix() method to get this object. Various pre-processing actions can be applied in this method such as removeNumbers, removePunctuation, removeSparseTerms, removeStopwords, stemWords, stripWhitespace, toLower, and weighting=weightTf.

3. Create a container object. This object contains train and test sets of matrices which will be used as inputs to the machine learning algorithms with the labels. This object will be used in the subsequent steps of analyzing data. For this we use the create_container() function.

4. Train the models. We train specific models using the container and a specific algorithm or list of supported algorithms as inputs. RTextTools provides two convenient methods for this purpose: train_model() and train_models(). The former method models only one algorithm at a time, whereas the latter method models a list of algorithms. To get a list of algorithms supported, use the print_algorithms() function.

5. Classify the data. In this step, we use the trained model to classify the data in the test sets. For this we use a function, classify_model() or classify_models(), based on the number of algorithms we have used to train our models.

6. Find the analytics. This is one of the most important steps. Here we understand the results and the users can get the information on various parameters, such as by label, by algorithm, by document, and an ensemble summary. For performing this action, we have a function, create_analytics(). The amount of information provided by this method depends on the virgin flag: if the flag is true that means the test set is classified , if it is false it means the test set is unclassified .The summary provides a complete view of each algorithm's performance for each unique label in the classified data. This includes information such as precision, recall, f-scores, and the accuracy of each algorithm's results as compared to the actual data.

We can also understand other important parameters such as algorithm accuracy and ensemble agreement, where predictions are same when we use different algorithms. We can use `create_ensembleSummary()` for this purpose. We can use cross-validation (n-fold cross validation) to calculate the accuracy of each algorithm and exporting the labeled data.

For the purpose of understanding this package hands on, let us take our previous example of mail datasets. For simplicity, we are reading the text files into a corpus converting the corpus into a data frame and adding the labels to the last column of the data frame.

It is important that, when you are doing text analysis, all your categories/labels are in text format. It should be converted to numeric. Otherwise, it will fail in the `create_analytics()` call.

```
#Load the obama speech:
obamaCorpus <- Corpus(DirSource(directory = "D:/R/Chap 6/Speeches/
obama" , encoding="UTF-8"))

obamaDataFrame<-data.frame(text=unlist(sapply(obamaCorpus, `[`,
"content")),stringsAsFactors=F)

obama.df <- cbind(obamaDataFrame , rep("obama" ,
nrow(obamaDataFrame)))
colnames(obama.df)[ncol(obama.df)] <- "name"

#Load the romney speech:
romneyCorpus <- Corpus(DirSource(directory = "D:/R/Chap 6/Speeches/
romney" , encoding="UTF-8"))

romneyDataFrame<-data.frame(text=unlist(sapply(romneyCorpus, `[`,
"content")),stringsAsFactors=F)

romney.df <- cbind(romneyDataFrame , rep("romney" ,
nrow(romneyDataFrame)))
colnames(romney.df)[ncol(romney.df)] <- "name"

# Combine both the speeches into one big data frame:
speech.df <- rbind(obama.df, romney.df)

speech_matrix <- create_matrix(speech.df["text"], language="english",
weighting=tm::weightTfIdf)

speech_container <- create_container(speech_matrix,as.
numeric(factor(speech.df$name)),trainSize=1:2000, testSize=2001:3857,
virgin=FALSE)
```

```
speech_model <- train_model(speech_container,"SVM")

speech_results <- classify_model(speech_container,speech_model)

speech_analytics <- create_analytics(speech_container, speech_results)

speech_score_summary <- create_scoreSummary(speech_container, speech_
results)

summary(speech_results)
SVM_LABEL     SVM_PROB
 1:1554    Min.    :0.5000
 2: 303    1st Qu.:0.7556
           Median :0.8715
           Mean   :0.8118
           3rd Qu.:0.8715
           Max.   :1.0000
  summary(speech_score_summary)
SVM_LABEL     BEST_LABEL      BEST_PROB      NUM_AGREE
 1:1554    Min.   :1.000    1:1554     Min.   :1
 2: 303    1st Qu.:1.000    2: 303     1st Qu.:1
           Median :1.000               Median :1
           Mean   :1.163               Mean   :1
           3rd Qu.:1.000               3rd Qu.:1
           Max.   :2.000               Max.   :1
summary(speech_analytics)
ENSEMBLE SUMMARY
      n-ENSEMBLE COVERAGE n-ENSEMBLE RECALL
n >= 1
                    1               0.16
ALGORITHM PERFORMANCE
SVM_PRECISION    SVM_RECALL    SVM_FSCORE
             1             1             1


#Let's try out multiple algorithms on the same data frame:
speech_multi_models <- train_models(speech_container,
algorithms=c("MAXENT","SVM"))

speech_multi_results <- classify_models(speech_container,speech_multi_
models)

speech_multi_analytics <- create_analytics(speech_container, speech_
multi_results)
```

```
ensemble_summary <- create_ensembleSummary(speech_multi_analytics@
document_summary)

precisionRecallSummary <- create_precisionRecallSummary(speech_
container, speech_multi_results, b_value = 1)

scoreSummary <- create_scoreSummary(speech_container, speech_multi_
results)

recall_acc <- recall_accuracy (speech_multi_analytics@
document_summary$MANUAL_CODE,speech_multi_analytics@document_
summary$MAXENTROPY_LABEL)

summary(speech_multi_results)
MAXENTROPY_LABEL MAXENTROPY_PROB   SVM_LABEL      SVM_PROB
  1:1578          Min.   :0.5000   1:1558      Min.   :0.5000
  2: 279          1st Qu.:0.5000   2: 299      1st Qu.:0.7537
                  Median :0.5084               Median :0.8689
                  Mean   :0.6933               Mean   :0.8092
                  3rd Qu.:0.9561               3rd Qu.:0.8689
                  Max.   :1.0000               Max.   :1.0000
summary(recall_acc)
   Min. 1st Qu.  Median   Mean 3rd Qu.   Max.
 0.1502  0.1502  0.1502 0.1502  0.1502 0.1502
summary(scoreSummary)
MAXENTROPY_LABEL SVM_LABEL   BEST_LABEL     BEST_PROB   NUM_AGREE
  1:1578          1:1558    Min.   :1.000   1:1584    Min.   :1.000
  2: 279          2: 299    1st Qu.:1.000   2: 273    1st Qu.:2.000
                            Median :1.000             Median :2.000
                            Mean   :1.147             Mean   :1.933
                            3rd Qu.:1.000             3rd Qu.:2.000
                            Max.   :2.000             Max.   :2.000
summary(precisionRecallSummary)
 SVM_PRECISION   SVM_RECALL    SVM_FSCORE  MAXENTROPY_PRECISION
MAXENTROPY_RECALL MAXENTROPY_FSCORE
 Min.   :1     Min.   :1     Min.   :1    Min.   :1          Min.
:1        Min.   :1
 1st Qu.:1     1st Qu.:1     1st Qu.:1    1st Qu.:1          1st
Qu.:1        1st Qu.:1
 Median :1     Median :1     Median :1    Median :1          Median
:1        Median :1
 Mean   :1     Mean   :1     Mean   :1    Mean   :1          Mean
:1        Mean   :1
 3rd Qu.:1     3rd Qu.:1     3rd Qu.:1    3rd Qu.:1          3rd
Qu.:1        3rd Qu.:1
```

```
    Max.   :1      Max.    :1     Max.    :1     Max.    :1                Max.
    :1            Max.    :1
summary(speech_multi_analytics)
ENSEMBLE SUMMARY
        n-ENSEMBLE COVERAGE n-ENSEMBLE RECALL
n >= 1                 1.00                 0.15
n >= 2                 0.93                 0.13


ALGORITHM PERFORMANCE
        SVM_PRECISION              SVM_RECALL              SVM_FSCORE
MAXENTROPY_PRECISION        MAXENTROPY_RECALL        MAXENTROPY_FSCORE
                    1                       1                        1
1                           1                       1
```

Model evaluation

There are multiple metrics for model evaluation in case of binary class classification problems in machine learning. These metrics help us evaluate the performance of the model and also in the parameter tuning process.

Confusion matrix

How can we describe the performance of a classifier, that is, when we have trained a model and have test data which has all the values, how can we assess the classifier's performance using the test data? The confusion matrix comes to our rescue. In the field of machine learning, the confusion matrix is used to assess the performance of the classifier. This matrix is also called the error matrix or contingency table. The confusion matrix has a simple table structure which aids the user to visualize the performance of an algorithm and it is very simple to understand. This type of analysis is generally used in supervised learning.

Let me take the confusion matrix from my spam classifier. The following is the output of the confusion matrix from the classifier. The confusion matrix was created using a method:

```
confusionMatrix ( prediction, testOutcome);
```

This method is available in the R package Caret.

The following confusion matrix shows the classifier performance. It tells if the classifier correctly detected spam to spam and ham to ham.

N = 2068		Predicted Class	
Ham		Spam	
Actual Class	Ham	855	1
	Spam	626	586

Let's dive deeply into the terminologies of the confusion matrix. The column specifies the actual class and the row specifies the predicted class.

- **True Positives(TP)** : These are the mails that were ham and were detected as ham

- **True Negatives(TN)** : These are the mails that were spam and were detected as spam

- **False Positives(FP)** : These are the mails that were ham but were detected as spam

- **False Negatives(FN)** : These are the mails that were spam but were detected as ham

We can visualize the preceding pointers in a table format for better understanding as follows:

N = 2068		Predicted Class	
Ham		Spam	
Actual Class	**Ham**	855(TP)	1(FP)
	Spam	626(FN)	586(TN)

A lot of important information can be derived from the confusion matrix.

The *True Positive Rate*, also called sensitivity, can be derived using the following formula:

True Positive Rate = $\frac{TP}{TP+FN}$

The *True Negative Rate* is also called specificity:

True Positive Rate = $\frac{TN}{TP+FP}$

Precision can be calculated using:

Precision = $\frac{TP}{TP+FP}$

Negative predictive value = $\frac{TN}{TN+FN}$

Fallout Rate = $\frac{FP}{FP+TN}$

Accuracy = $\frac{TP+TN}{(TP+FN)+(FP+TN)}$

The *F1* score can be calculated using, this is a Harmonic mean of sensitivity and Precision:

F1 = $\frac{2TP}{2TP+FN+FP}$

ROC curve

Receiver Operating Characteristics Curve (ROC) is the plot between True Positive Rate and False Positive Rate of classification in a binary class problem, such as instance opinion mining, where classes are positive sentiments and negative sentiments. This curve depicts the performance of a classifier without taking the class distribution into the context.

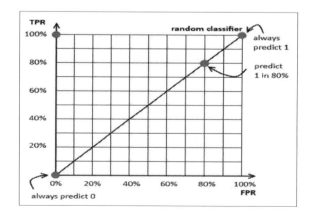

```
install.packages('ROCR')
```

```
library(ROCR)
data(ROCR.simple)
```

```
pred <- prediction( ROCR.simple$predictions, ROCR.simple$labels)
perf <- performance(pred,"tpr","fpr")
plot(perf,colorize=TRUE)
lines(x=c(0, 1), y=c(0, 1), col="black")
```

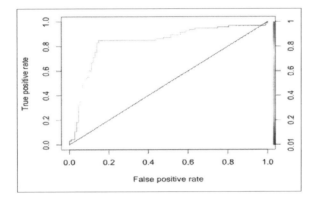

Precision-recall

Let's say we have a collection of documents, from which we have to retrieve documents that match a certain criteria. We query the collection based on that criteria and we get a list of matching documents. Our retrieval mechanism A returned 200 documents, out of which 60 were relevant, while another retrieval mechanism returned 100 documents, out of which 30 were relevant. We have the prior information that there are overall 400 relevant documents in the collection. How do we decide which of the mechanisms worked better? We need to look into the false positives and false negatives here. Recall in this context means the ratio of the number of relevant documents retrieved to the overall number of relevant documents in the collection.

Precision means the ratio of the number of relevant documents retrieved to the overall number of documents retrieved. So, for this example, Mechanism *A* has a recall of *60/400= 0.15* and precision of *60/200=0.3*; while *B* has a recall of *30/400=0.075* and precision of *30/100=0.30*. Clearly, Mechanism A worked better, as it has a high recall rate while the precision is the same for both.

```
perf1 <- performance(pred, "prec", "rec")
plot(perf1,colorize=TRUE)
```

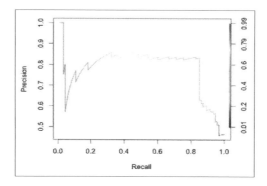

```
perf1 <- performance(pred, "sens", "spec")
plot(perf1,colorize=TRUE)
```

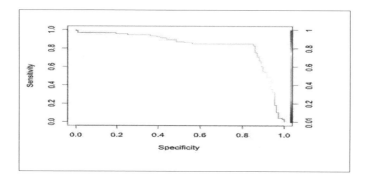

Bias–variance trade-off and learning curve

It has been observed that non-linear classifiers are usually more powerful than the linear classifiers for text classification problems. But, that does not necessarily imply that a non-linear classifier is the solution to each text classification problem. It is quite interesting to note that there does not exist any optimal learning algorithm that can be universally applicable. Thus, the algorithm selection becomes quite a pivotal part of any modeling exercise. Also, the complexity of a model should not entirely be assumed by the fact that it is a linear or non-linear classifier; there are multiple other aspects of a modeling process, which can lead to complexity in the model, such as feature selection, regularization, and so on.

The error components in a learning model can be categorized broadly as irreducible errors and reducible errors. Irreducible errors are caused by inherent variability in a system; not much can be done about this component. A reducible error component is the one which can be minimized to increase the prediction accuracy. It is very important to understand the phenomenon of bias and variance, the different error sources which lead to these components and the trade-off between them, in order to improve the model fitting process and come up with highly accurate models. In a classification model, bias and variance are the reducible error components that may prohibit the algorithm from being able to approximate on an unknown test data. The bias-variance tradeoff phenomenon is about trying to decrease these two errors simultaneously. Because of its presence, there is no universally optimal learning algorithm. In an ideal world, a learning method should not only be able to extract the regularities in the training data but also be capable of generalizing over an unobserved dataset. But because of bias-variance tradeoff, this is literally impossible to achieve.

High bias in a model typically implies a simpler model, which barely fits the data; or under-fits the data and loses out on vital regularities in the training data. On the other hand, a high variance would mean the model captures the regularities in the training data really well. This means it is able to fit the training data really well but does not generalize well on unobserved instances, which is a typical case of over-fitting on the training data. Low bias models typically carry a lot of complexity, which for sure fits the training data well, but despite the high complexity it might still not be able to predict well on unseen instances because of the added noise component that comes with increased complexity.

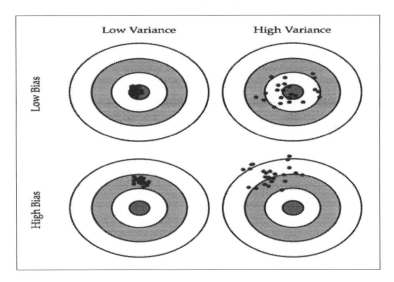

Bias-variance decomposition

As we learnt in the last segment, there are two components of error in a learning model: reducible and irreducible components. An expected error on any unobserved instance can be decomposed as:

$$E\left[\left(y-\hat{f}(x)\right)^2\right] = Bias\left[\hat{f}(x)\right]^2 + Var\left[\hat{f}(x)\right] + \sigma^2$$

Where:

$$Bias\left[\hat{f}(x)\right] = E\left[\hat{f}(x)\right] - f(x)$$

And:

$$Var\left[\hat{f}(x)\right] = E\left[\left(\hat{f}(x) - E\left[\hat{f}(x)\right]\right)^2\right]$$

If we sample our training data multiple times, it is quite obvious we will get to learn a different hypothesis most of the time, due to the underlying randomness in the training data. Thus, the resultant learner will have a range of predictions. Bias is the measure of the difference between the prediction and the expected value in general. High bias means, the average prediction is substantially far away from the expected or true value. It tends to decrease with the added complexity in the model.

An error due to variance is the measure of variability in predictions caused by multiple realization of the model. Let's say, we go through the model building process across the entire training set multiple times, and observe the variability in the predictions for a specific instance across all the models. The error due to variance is the difference between what is expected to be learnt from a dataset and what is actually learnt from it. It decreases with the decrease in complexity of the model, as shown in the following diagram:

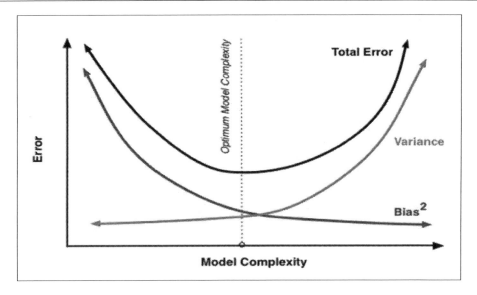

Learning curve

The learning curve is a plot between the training data used against the training and test error, plotted to diagnose the learning algorithm in order to minimize the reducible errors. The following example is a typical case of high variance:

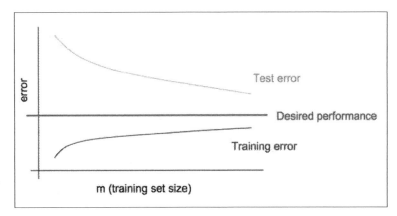

The following diagram is a typical case of high bias. The training error and test error are too close and thus the model has under-fit. We need to choose a more complex algorithm which can fit well on this data and provide us with better generalization ability.

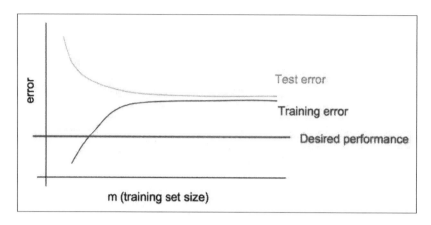

Dealing with reducible error components

High bias:

- Add more features
- Apply a more complex model
- Use less instances to train
- Reduce regularization

High variance:

- Conduct feature selection and use less features
- Get more training data
- Use regularization to help overcome the issues due to complex models

Cross validation

Cross-validation is an important step in the model validation and evaluation process. It is a technique to validate the performance of a model before we apply it on an unobserved dataset. It is not advised to use the full training data to train the model, because in such a case we would have no idea how the model is going to perform in practice. As we learnt in the previous section, a good learner should be able to generalize well on an unseen dataset; that can happen only if the model is able to extract and learn the underlying patterns or relations among the dependent and independent attributes. If we train the model on the full training data and apply the same on a test data, it is very likely that we will have very low prediction errors on the training set while the accuracy on the test set is significantly low. This would mean that the model is overfitting. The classifier did not learn from the data, but it just remembered a specific interaction of independent variables to the class variable. Thus it was not able to generalize well on the unseen test data. The scenarios where we have a fewer number of instances or a high number of parameters is when it is very likely that the model may overfit. How do we handle it?

Cross-validation helps in validating the model fit on an artificially created test data, which is kept aside during the training process, that is, it is restricted from the learner to train the model on. It is very common to divide the annotated data into two parts: training set and cross-validation or holdout set, typically in the ration of 60%-40% or 70%-30% of the whole data. The training is performed on the training set and the trained model is used to predict on the cross-validation set. If the model performs well on the training data but the accuracy falls down significantly on the cross-validation set, it's a typical case of overfitting.

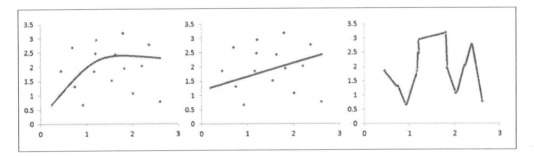

Some of the other model validation methods are:

- Leave-one-out
- k-fold
- Repeated hold
- Bootstrap
- Stratified

Leave-one-out

Leave-one-out is a variant of the `Leave-p-out` method of cross-validation where *p=1*. In this method, the entire instance except for one is left out during the model training process and the model is tested on the left out instance. This is done exhaustively for all the instances, and the error rate is calculated. In simple words, the algorithm leaves out each instance in turn, validates the hypotheses generated by training the model on the remaining instances, and stores the correctness of the model in binary form. Once this step runs for all the instances, the results for all the iteration (typically many instances are available in data) is averaged to come up with the final estimate of the error.

There are a few obvious benefits of this method. In this method, the largest possible set of data is used for training, which in an ideal scenario, should increase the classifier accuracy. This mechanism of sampling data is unbiased, it is deterministic in nature, and does not involve random sampling.

One glaring concern associated with this method is the computational cost. Leave-one-out can even be called **n-fold cross-validation**, where *n* is the number of instances in the data. The process repeats itself *n* number of times, leaving one instance out in turn and training for the remaining instance. The process completes only after the error is estimated in the context of each instance being left out in the training process once. This makes this method computationally very expensive. The other issue associated to this mechanism is that we can never have stratified samples in training if we perform leave-one-out sampling. We have not yet learnt about k-fold and stratified; these concerns can be understood better after we learn about all the cross-validation methods.

k-Fold

For all practical purposes, we need to evaluate our model both on unbiased data as well as a variation of datasets. A good way of to get this estimate is **k-fold cross-validation**. In this process, we first randomly divide the dataset in *k* parts, each part has almost the same number of data points. Out of these *k* parts one part is retained as the test data and the remaining parts are used for training purposes. The entire process is repeated *K* number of times and during each pass exactly one part is held out for testing. All the results can be averaged to get the overall error rate. One upside to this method is that all the parts are used for training and each part is used for validating at least once. The standard way is to use **10-fold cross-validation** and compute the overall error estimate. It's debatable if this thumb rule applies universally, although there are mathematical proofs to back the claim that *10* in most of the cases is a good approximation of the number of folds to be chosen. k-fold cross-validation may produce different outcomes when run on the same dataset using the same model because of the variations. Although stratification reduces variation to a good extent there are still some differences in the outcomes. It's a common practice to apply k-fold cross validation *k* number of times, which means the model would run *k2* number of times, on the training data which would be *(k-1/k)* th the size of the full data. This makes it very obvious that it's a computationally expensive process.

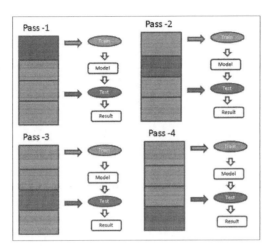

Some R Packages that can be used for k-fold cross-validation.

The R package, cvTools Function cvFit() can be used to predict the errors of a model using k-fold cross-validation:

```
install.packages("cvTools")
install.packages("robustbase")
data("coleman")
fit <- lmrob(Y ~ ., data=coleman)
cvFit(fit, data = coleman, y = coleman$Y, cost = rtmspe, K = 5, R =
10, costArgs = list(trim = 0.1), seed = 1234)

5-fold CV results:
      CV
0.9867381

install.packages("boot")
cv.glm(data, glmfit, cost, K)
```

The parameters to the `glm()` function are described as follows:

- `glmfit`: Results of a generalized linear model fitted to data
- `data`: A matrix or data frame containing the data
- `cost`: A function of two vector arguments specifying the cost function for the cross-validation
- `K`: The number of groups into which the data should be split to estimate the cross-validation prediction error

Bootstrap

Both the cross-validation and bootstrapping methods are used to estimate the generalization errors in a model by performing validation on resampled data. In the bootstrap sampling procedure, we will sample the dataset with replacement. In all the preceding methods when a sample was picked form the dataset it was not replaced, that is, the same instance once selected could not be used again. If the model is learning on a sample that has reputation then the results of the learning may be different. This is the idea behind bootstrap cross-validation. Since we are sampling the data with replacement, as a result some of the instances would occur more than once in a sample wherein some of them may never appear. What is the probability of any specific instance not being picked for the training set?

If the dataset has n number of instances, the probability of a specific instance to be picked for training is $1/n$ and thus the probability of this instance not being picked up comes to be $1-1/n$. This is the probability of the specific instance I not being picked for a specific iteration. The probability of any specific instance never being picked in any of the samples comes out to be $(1-1/n)n$ which is approximately equal to $1/e$, approximately equal to 0.367.

This implies, for a sufficiently large dataset, approximately 63% of the data would appear in the training set while about 37% of the data would never feature in training samples and thus it can be used at the test set.

Stratified

In stratified sampling, another probability sampling technique in which the entire dataset is divided into separate groups, these groups are called **strata**. A random sample is drawn from each group. It has many advantages over just dividing the datasets into test and train sets, as the data is distributed evenly across samples, which will help the model to learn most of the patterns in the provided sample. One thing to keep in mind is, if the datasets have overlapping strata then the probability of a particular data point being picked might increase.

The caret package in R has a method, `trainControl()`, which supports various sampling methods:

- `boot`
- `boot632`
- `cv`
- `repeatedcv`
- `LOOCV`
- `LGOCV`
- `adaptive_cv`
- `adaptive_boot`

For more information refer to `https://cran.r-project.org/web/packages/caret/caret.pdf`

Summary

In this chapter, we learned about text classification methods and their implementation in R language. We learnt how to use classifiers to build applications such as spam filter, topic models, and so on. We also looked into the model evaluation and validation methods. In the coming chapters, we will take up more practical examples to utilize the tools and knowledge gained in the previous chapters to mine and extract insights from social media. We will also look into different distributed text mining methods to help applications build in R to scale up for high dimensional data.

7
Entity Recognition

Extracting information out of unstructured text data is a tedious process, because of the complex nature of natural language. Even after advancements in the field of **Natural language processing (NLP)**, we are far from the point where any unrestricted text can be analyzed and the meaning can be extracted for general purposes. However, if we just focus on a specific set of questions, we can extract a significant amount of information from the text data. Named entity recognition helps identify the important entities in a text, to be able to derive the meaning from the unstructured data. It is a vital component of NLP applications, for example, question-answering systems, product discovery on e-commerce websites, and so on.

In this chapter, we will cover the following topics:

- Entity extraction
- Coreference and relationship extraction
- Sentence boundary detection
- Named entity recognition

Entity extraction

The process of extracting information from unstructured documents is called information extraction. In today's world, most of the data produced over the internet is semi-structured or unstructured; this data is mostly in a human-understandable format, what we call natural language, so most of the time, natural language processing comes into play during information extraction. Entity recognition is a sub process in the chain of information extraction process. NER is one of the important and vital parts of the information extraction process. NER is sometimes also called entity extraction or entity chunking .The main job of NER is to extract the rigid designators in the document and classify these elements in the text to a predefined category. The named entity extractor has a set of predefined categories such as the following:

- persons
- organizations
- locations
- time
- money
- percentages
- dates

Given an unstructured document, NER will annotate the block or extract the relevant features. Consider a sample text as shown here:

> *"IBM developed AI software in 2006. It named after IBM's first CEO and industrialist Thomas J. Watson. Watson won $1 million in Jeopardy game."*

After processing through the NER algorithm, the text is annotated with various predefined categories as shown here:

> *"IBM(Company) developed a AI software named Watson in 2006(Date). It named after IBM's(Company) first CEO and industrialist Thomas J. Watson (Person). Watson won $1(Money) million in Jeopardy game."*

While annotating the given document, there may be words that may have a different meaning based on the context; for example, in the preceding example, Watson is the name of software but it can also be the name of a person. Let's consider one more simple example as follows:

> *Tim Cook is the CEO of Apple.*

In the preceding sentence, Apple is the name of a company and not a fruit. NER algorithms can use contextual information to find out the right tag for a given entity.

NER is a challenging task; it is basically divided into two parts:

- Identification of named entities
- Classification of named entities

There are various approaches followed to solve the NER challenge. Following are a couple of approaches followed to develop NER systems.

The rule-based approach

These methods are based on linguistic rules and grammar-based techniques. Grammar-based systems are more accurate but need lot of work to be done by experts in computational linguists. Some of the rule-based NER systems are:

- GATE
- CIMPLE
- System T

Machine learning

This type of solution is based on statically models. This kind of NER system needs a huge amount of annotated corpus, which is called training data. The algorithm process the annotated corpus learns or create rules and builds a model to further identify entities in new documents. Supervised learning is one approach followed to build NER systems. Annotating a large corpus is a challenging and time-consuming task. Some of the statistical algorithms used for supervised learning are:

- Maximum entropy models
- Hidden Markov models
- Support vector machines
- Conditional random fields

Semi-supervised learning is gaining momentum in building NER systems since it requires less human intervention and solves the problem of large annotated corpus availability. This kind of technique basically has a sentence boundary detector, tokenizer, and part of speech tagger.

In unsupervised learning, we try to infer the named entity by looking into a cluster which is built under a similar context. This approach uses some lexical databases such as word net to identify the named entity types.

There are various NLP frameworks available to perform various tasks in natural language processing:

- Apache OpenNLP
- Stanford NLP
- LingPipe

In this chapter, we will learn how to invoke the Apache OpenNLP library through R using various R libraries such as *openNLP*, *rJava*, and *NLP*.

Apache OpenNLP is a Java-based framework. It has implementation to machine learning algorithms that can be used for natural language processing. It has supporting APIs to perform for some of the important steps in natural language processing, such as:

- Part of speech tagging
- Sentence boundary detection
- Tokenization
- Chunking
- Parsing
- Named entity extraction
- Coreference resolution

It has implementations to algorithms such as maximum entropy and perceptron-based machine learning. Using various components from Apache OpenNLP, we can build an end-to-end language-processing pipeline. All the functionality for various methods is exposed as application programming interface. Each component generally has a training module and a testing/predicting module. Let's get an understanding the functionality provided by OpenNLP.

Sentence boundary detection

Sentence boundary detection is an important step in NLP and an essential problem to be solved before analyzing the text for further use in information extraction, word tokenization, part of speech tagging, and so on. A sentence is a basic unit of text. Tough SBD has been solved to a good extent, extracting sentences from a text document is not a simple process. Sentence boundary detection is language dependent since the sentence termination character in each language may be different. This can be done using a machine learning approach by training a model rule-based approach. If we consider the English language then the simple set of rules which can give us a fairly accurate results are:

- Text is terminated by a period (.)
- Text is terminated by an exclamation mark (!)
- Text is terminated by a question mark (?)

Consider the following example:

NLP is a vast topic. Lots of research has been done in this field.

When we apply the preceding set of rules, we can extract all the sentences easily. We can see there are two sentences. Sometimes, due to the way these characters are used in English, sentence boundary detection becomes a tricky task. Consider the following example:

Mr. James is expert in NLP. James lives in the U.S.A.

When we apply the preceding set of rules, we get four sentences since there are four periods. The human brain can understand that Mr. is a prefix so the period doesn't mean the end of a sentence and U.S.A is an abbreviation and the period here does not mean the end of a sentence because it has some contextual information. Some of the common challenges while detecting sentences are abbreviations, use of punctuation, quotes within a sentence, and special characters in text such as tweets, but how can we make machine understand this? We will need a complex set of rules to understand abbreviations, prefixes, and quotes so, based on this, we can add two more rules such as:

- Abbreviations do not come before period.
- Numbers do not occur after period.

But how do you detect abbreviations? Are the words with all caps abbreviations? We can use a list of domain-specific abbreviations; these rules keep on growing as the complexity and the context of the text changes. Some of these subtle differences in the use of punctuation can make SBD tricky.

The examples shows the abbreviations causing ambiguity in SBD: in the first sentence, there are no period characters between the letters in the abbreviation NASA, and in the second sentence, NASA has periods in between:

> *"Mark is an astronaut in NASA."*

> *"Mark is an astronaut in N.A.S.A."*

Quotes inside a sentence or sentence within a sentence:

> *Alien said, "Welcome to MARS"*

An exclamation mark is a part of a word not the end of sentence:

> *"Yahoo!"*

We can use double exclamation marks but that does not mean there are two sentences:

> *"Congratulations!!"*

In the following sentence, an ellipsis is used as a termination character:

> *"The story continued ..."*

Here it's not the end of the sentence:

> *"I wasn't really ...well"*

Character encoding can also complicate the problems since some punctuation is treated as one character in certain encodings and as multiple characters in a different encoding.

Let's do a simple SBD in R using the OpenNLP package.

Load the required libraries; these libraries are already been installed:

```
library(rJava)
library(NLP)
library(openNLP)
```

We will consider a simple text and extract the sentences out of it:

```
simpleText <- "Text Mining is a interesting field. Mr. Paul Is a good
programmer. He loves watching football. He lives in U.S.A."
```

Let's convert a character array into string:

```
simpleText_str <- as.String(simpleText)
```

Let's use the `Maxent_Sent_Token_Annotator()` method; this generates an annotator which calculates sentence annotations using the Apache OpenNLP `Maxent` sentence detector. This method is just an interface to the actual API exposed by Apache OpenNLP, This method can also take the following parameters as input:

- `language`
- `probs`
- `model`

If you don't provide the parameters, then the defaults are:

- `language = "en"`
- `probs = FALSE`
- `model = NULL`

It will use the `en-sent.bin` when we initialize this with defaults:

```
sent_token_annotator <- Maxent_Sent_Token_Annotator()
```

We use the annotate function from *NLP* R package; it calculates annotations by iterating over the given annotators and applying them to the input text, the output is merged values of the newly computed annotations with the current ones:

```
annotated_sentence <- annotate(simpleText_str,sent_token_annotator)
```

Let's inspect the value inside the annotated sentence:

```
annotated_sentence
```

The output is as follows:

```
id type      start end features
 1 sentence      1  35
 2 sentence     37  66
 3 sentence     68  94
 4 sentence     96 113
```

From the preceding output snapshot, we can see there are four sentences; it also provides the information on the start and end of each sentence.

Let's use the `MaxEnt` Sentence Annotator using the parameter `"probs = TRUE"` and see the difference in output:

```
annotated_sentence_prob <- annotate(simpleText_str, Maxent_Sent_Token_
Annotator(probs = TRUE))
```

```
id type      start end features
1 sentence      1  35 prob=0.9984942
2 sentence     37  66 prob=0.9997188
3 sentence     68  94 prob=0.9999296
4 sentence     96 113 prob=0.6876867
```

The output has a features column which shows the confidence of the sentences detected. In order to get all the sentences from the string, we can use the following code:

```
simpleText_str[annotated_sentence]
```

```
"Text Mining is a interesting field."
"Mr. Paul Is a good programmer."
"He loves watching football."
"He lives in U.S.A."
```

We just saw how to invoke the `MaxEnt` sentence boundary detector from the R package, now let's understand what is happening under the hood, what Java code actually gets called, and what it actually does.

Apache OpenNLP can detect that a punctuation marks at the end of a sentence. The model used in OpenNLP is trained on data where white space follows sentence termination punctuation. That is, *a sentence is defined as the longest white space trimmed character sequence between two punctuation marks. The first non-whitespace character is assumed to be the beginning of a sentence, and the last non-whitespace character is assumed to be a sentence end;* this is a good standard in English orthography. English sentence detectors are trained to differentiate between sentence termination punctuation and punctuation used in between the sentence in abbreviations and so on.

Let's look a sample of Java code, used for sentence detection using Apache OpenNLP

We will assume all the required libraries are on your `java` class path. `import` statement to get the relevant class files and their methods:

```
import java.io.FileInputStream;
import java.io.IOException;
import java.io.InputStream;
import opennlp.tools.sentdetect.SentenceDetectorME;
import opennlp.tools.sentdetect.SentenceModel;
import opennlp.tools.util.InvalidFormatException;


public class SentenceDetector {

public static void DetectSentence() throws InvalidFormatException,
    IOException {

String text = "Text Mining is a interesting field. Mr. Paul Is a good
programmer. He loves watching football. He lives in U.S.A.";
```

Now let's load a model:

1. This model is created by using training data; we will read the file `en-sent.bin` which is the OpenNPL pre-trained model for the English language:

   ```
   InputStream is = new FileInputStream("en-sent.bin");
   ```

2. We need to create a new object of the `SentenceModel` class using the `bin` file loaded into the input stream in the previous line:

   ```
   SentenceModel model = new SentenceModel(is);
   ```

3. We will instantiate a `SentenceDetectirME` instance; it is a sentence detector class for splitting up raw text into sentences. It uses a maximum entropy model to evaluate end-of-sentence characters in a string to determine if they are the actual end of a sentence:

   ```
   SentenceDetectorME sdetector = new SentenceDetectorME(model);
   ```

4. Detect sentences in a string. The input for this is the actual text:

   ```
   String sentences[] = sdetector.sentDetect(text);
   ```

5. Print all the detected sentences to the console:

   ```
   for(String sentence : sentences){
   System.out.println(sentences);

   }
   ```

6. Clean up the resource:

```
is.close();
}

public static void main(String[] args) throws
InvalidFormatException, IOException {
```

7. Invoke the method to perform sentence detection:

```
    DetectSentence();
  }
}
```

8. The output after executing the preceding program is:

```
Problems  Console ⊠  Search  Progress  Debug  History
<terminated> ss [Java Application] C:\Program Files\Java\jdk1.8.0_40\jre\bin\javaw.
Text Mining is a interesting field.
Mr. Paul Is a good programmer.
He loves watching football.
He lives in U.S.A.
```

Some of the useful methods exposed by `SentenceDetectorME` class are:

- `getSentenceProbabilities()`: Returns the probabilities associated with the most recent calls to `sentDetect()`

- `sentDetect (String s)`: Detects sentences in a string

- `sentPosDetect (String s)`: Detects the position of the first words of sentences in a String

- `train (String, ObjectStream, SentenceDetectorFactory, TrainingParameters)`: Trains a new annotated text

So when we invoke an R code for SBD, it invokes the Java code as shown preceding under the hood and finally passes the output to the `Simple_Sent_Token_Annotator()` method for the *NLP* package which creates annotator objects.

We can obtain various pre-trained sentence boundary detection models for different languages from `http://opennlp.sourceforge.net/models-1.5/`:

- `en-sent.bin`
- `nl-sent.bin`
- `se-sent.bin`

We can train or create our own sentence boundary detector model by using the `train()` API exposed by `SentenceDetectorME` class. In order to achieve this, the training data must meet certain prerequisites. The data must be in OpenNLP Sentence Detector training format or it has to be converted into the OpenNLP Sentence Detector training format which is:

- One sentence per line
- Empty line indicates a document boundary
- Recommended to have an empty line every 10 sentences if the document boundary is unknown

Word token annotator

In order to tokenize the words in a document, we can use `Maxent_Word_Token_Annotator()` from the OpenNLP package; this method invokes the Apache OpenNLP `Maxent` tokenizer, which tokens the input text into tokens. Tokens are nothing but words, numbers, and punctuation. Apache OpenNLP has three different types of tokenizer:

- Whitespace tokenizer
- Simple tokenizer
- Maximum entropy tokenizer

Word tokenization is an important step in language processing; the tokenized output may be used in parsers, POS taggers, and entity extractor. When we use word "tokenizer" in OpenNLP, we have to first identify the sentence boundaries by using `Maxent_Sent_Token_Annotator()` and then the sentences are further tokenized into words.

Let's see how to execute `Maxent_Sent_Token_Annotator()` in R:

1. Load the required libraries; these libraries are already been installed:

   ```
   library(rJava)
   library(NLP)
   library(openNLP)
   ```

2. We will consider a simple text and extract the sentences out of it:

   ```
   simpleText <- "Text Mining is a interesting field. Mr. Paul Is a
   good programmer. He loves watching football. He lives in U.S.A."
   ```

3. Let's convert a character array into string and run a sentence annotation method; this is mandatory because Apache OpenNLP first tokenizes the sentences and then tokenizes the word in each sentence:

```
simpleText_str <- as.String(simpleText)
sent_token_annotator <- Maxent_Sent_Token_Annotator(probs=TRUE)
annotated_sentence <- annotate(simpleText_str,sent_token_
annotator)
```

Let's use the `Maxent_Word_Token_Annotator()` method; this generates an annotator which calculates sentence annotations using the Apache OpenNLP `Maxent` Word tokenizer. This method is just an interface to the actual API exposed by Apache OpenNLP. This method takes the following parameters:

- `language`
- `probs`
- `model`

If you don't provide the parameters, then the defaults are:

- `language = "en"`
- `probs = FALSE`
- `model = NULL`

It will use `en-token.bin` when we initialize this with defaults:

```
word_token_annotator <- Maxent_Word_Token_Annotator(probs=TRUE)
```

We use the annotate function from the *NLP* R package; it calculates annotations by iterating over the given annotators and applying them to the input text. The output is the merged values of the newly computed annotations with the current ones:

```
annotated_word <- annotate (simpleText_str, word_token_annotator,
annotated_sentence)
```

Let's inspect the value inside the annotated sentence, `annotated_word`:

```
id type      start end features
 1 sentence      1  35 prob=0.9984942, constituents=<<integer,7>>
 2 sentence     37  66 prob=0.9997188, constituents=<<integer,7>>
 3 sentence     68  94 prob=0.9999296, constituents=<<integer,5>>
 4 sentence     96 113 prob=0.6876867, constituents=<<integer,4>>
 5 word          1   4 prob=1
 6 word          6  11 prob=1
 7 word         13  14 prob=1
 8 word         16  16 prob=1
 9 word         18  28 prob=1
10 word         30  34 prob=0.9925478
11 word         35  35 prob=1
12 word         37  39 prob=0.9996333
13 word         41  44 prob=1
14 word         46  47 prob=1
15 word         49  49 prob=1
16 word         51  54 prob=1
17 word         56  65 prob=0.9402165
18 word         66  66 prob=1
19 word         68  69 prob=1
20 word         71  75 prob=1
21 word         77  84 prob=1
22 word         86  93 prob=0.9790488
23 word         94  94 prob=1
24 word         96  97 prob=1
25 word         99 103 prob=1
26 word        105 106 prob=1
27 word        108 113 prob=0.847792
```

The output provides lot of information, such as number of sentences, start and end of each sentence, probability of each sentence, number of words in the text, start and end of each word, and the probability of each word detected.

Let's inspect the output:

```
simpleText_str[annotated_word]
```

```
 [1] "Text Mining is a interesting field." "Mr. Paul Is a good programmer."  "He loves watching football."
 [4] "He lives in U.S.A."                  "Text"                           "Mining"
 [7] "is"                                  "a"                              "interesting"
[10] "field"                               "."                              "Mr."
[13] "Paul"                                "Is"                             "a"
[16] "good"                                "programmer"                     "."
[19] "He"                                  "loves"                          "watching"
[22] "football"                            "."                              "He"
[25] "lives"                               "in"                             "U.S.A."
```

First it lists all the sentences and then the words.

Let us look into what the Java APIs are that are exposed by Apache OpenNLP to perform the preceding process through a simple Java program:

1. Load the required libraries:

```java
import java.io.FileInputStream;
import java.io.IOException;
import java.io.InputStream;
import opennlp.tools.tokenize.Tokenizer;
import opennlp.tools.tokenize.TokenizerME;
import opennlp.tools.tokenize.TokenizerModel;
import opennlp.tools.util.InvalidFormatException;
public class WordTokenizer {
  public static void main(String[] args) throws
InvalidFormatException, IOException {

    Tokenize();
  }
  public static void Tokenize() throws InvalidFormatException,
IOException {
Input String
    String text = "Text Mining is a interesting field. Mr. Paul
Is a good programmer. He loves watching football. He lives in
U.S.A.";
```

2. We will load the pre-trained model provided by Apache OpenNLP:

```java
InputStream is = new FileInputStream("C:\\Users\\avia.ORADEV\\
Documents\\R\\win-library\\3.1\\openNLPdata\\models\\en-token.
bin");
```

3. We need to initialize the `TokenizerModel` class using the input stream:

```java
TokenizerModel model = new TokenizerModel(is);
```

4. We create a tokenizer. We instantiate a maximum entropy tokenizer. This tokenizer converts raw text into separated tokens. It uses Maximum Entropy to make its decisions:

```java
Tokenizer tokenizer = new TokenizerME(model);
```

5. Invoke tokenize method on the input text:

```java
String tokens[] = tokenizer.tokenize(text);

for (String token : tokens){
  System.out.println(token);
}
```

```
        is.close();
   }


}
```

6. The output of the programme is as follows. Now you know under the hood what APIs of OpenNLP are being called to do word tokenization:

Named entity recognition

Named entity recognition in a sub process in the natural language processing pipeline. We identify the names and numbers from the input document. The names can be names of a person or company, location numbers can be money or percentages, to name a few. In order to perform named entity recognition, we will use Apache OpenNLP TokenNameFinderModel API. In order to invoke the code from the R environment, we will use the OpenNLP R package:

1. Load the required libraries:

```
library(rJava)
library(NLP)
library(openNLP)
```

2. Create a sample text; we will extract the entities from this text:

```
txt <- " IBM is an MNC with headquarters in New York. Oracle is a
cloud company in California. James works in IBM. Oracle hired John
for cloud expertise. They give 100% to their profession"
```

3. We will convert it to string for processing:

```
txt_str <- as.String(txt)
```

4. We will process the text through the MaxEnt sentence token annotator and the MaxEnt word token annotator, both available in r packages and extensively discussed in the topics preceding. Let's create the respective annotator objects:

```
sent_token_annotator <- Maxent_Sent_Token_Annotator()
word_token_annotator <- Maxent_Word_Token_Annotator()
```

5. Pass the text and the annotator objects to the annotate function:

```
annotated_str <- annotate(txt_str, list(sent_token_annotator,
word_token_annotator))
```

First we will identify the company names present in the given text; for this, we will use the Maxent_Entity_Annotator() method from the OpenNLP R package. This method is an interface to the actual Apache OpenNLP's TokenNameFinderModel API. This method takes the following arguments:

- language
- kind
- probs
- model

If we don't provide any parameters, the defaults are considered, which are:

- language is "en"
- kind is "person"
- probs is FALSE
- model is NULL

The default model used to train the model is en-ner-organization.bin:

```
entity_annotator_org <-Maxent_Entity_Annotator(language = "en", kind =
"organization", probs = FALSE, model = NULL)
```

After creating the organization entity annotator object, we can use it in the annotate function to annotate the sample text:

```
annotated_org_val <- annotate(txt_str, entity_annotator_org,
annotated_str)
```

Let's see the results of annotation:

```
annotated_org_val
```

```
id type      start end features
 1 sentence     1  44 constituents=<<integer,10>>
 2 sentence    46  85 constituents=<<integer,8>>
 3 sentence    87 105 constituents=<<integer,5>>


      .   .   .   .
      .   .   .   .
      .   .   .   .


 9 word         11  13
41 word        164 168
42 word        170 179
43 entity        1   3 kind=organization
44 entity       46  51 kind=organization
45 entity      102 104 kind=organization
46 entity      107 112 kind=organization
```

If we look at the output, we can see from the given text it has identified four organization names. It also specified the start and end of the organization entity.

We can pass `probs=TRUE` and get the probability or the confidence measure of the identified entity. We will see the values at the location which are marked as organization:

```
txt_str[annotated_org_val]
```

```
[1] "IBM is an MNC with headquarters in New York." "Oracle is a cloud company in California."
[3] "James works in IBM."                           "Oracle hired John for cloud expertise."
[5] "They give 100% to their profession"            "IBM"


            .    .    .    .    .
            .    .    .    .    .
            .    .    .    .    .


[39] "%"                                             "to"
[41] "their"                                         "profession"
[43] "IBM"                                           "Oracle"
[45] "IBM"                                           "Oracle"
```

We can see at that at positions 43, 44, 45, 46, there are organization names.

So what Java code is getting executed when we call the `Maxent_Entity_Annotator()` method of OpenNLP package in R? In order to understand that, we will look into the code and APIs from Apache OpenNLP which help us to perform named entity recognition:

1. Load the required packages:

```
import java.io.FileInputStream;
import java.io.IOException;
import java.io.InputStream;
import java.util.Arrays;
import opennlp.tools.namefind.NameFinderME;
import opennlp.tools.namefind.TokenNameFinderModel;
import opennlp.tools.sentdetect.SentenceDetectorME;
import opennlp.tools.sentdetect.SentenceModel;
import opennlp.tools.tokenize.TokenizerME;
import opennlp.tools.tokenize.TokenizerModel;
import opennlp.tools.util.InvalidFormatException;
import opennlp.tools.util.Span;
```

2. Create a class and a main function to invoke the actual code:

```
public class OrganizationFinder {
   public static void main(String[] args) throws
InvalidFormatException,
      IOException {
    findOrg();
   }
```

3. Create a function that identifies the organization names:

```
private static void findOrg() throws InvalidFormatException,
IOException {
```

4. The same sample text which we use in our R code:

```
String txt = "IBM is an MNC with headquarters in New York. Oracle
is a cloud company in California. James works in IBM. Oracle hired
John for cloud expertise. They give 100% to their profession";
```

Before going into the coding, let me brief you about the steps necessary to perform named entity recognition using Apache OpenNLP.

The pseudo-code:

- Process the text with a sentence tokenizer; this will identify the sentences from the given text
- Process the tokenized sentence through a word tokenizer; this will identify the words from the given sentence
- Process this tokenized array to the name finder API to get the list of names

Read the pre-trained word detector model `en-token.bin` provided by Apache OpenNLP:

1. Now initialize a `TokenizerME` model using the same:

   ```
   InputStream token_is = new FileInputStream(" \\openNLPdata\\
   models\\en-token.bin");
   ```

2. Initialize the `TokenizerModel` class using the `InputStream` created preceding:

   ```
   TokenizerModel token_model = new TokenizerModel(token_is);
   ```

3. Clean up resources:

   ```
   token_is.clo12/20/2016se();
   ```

4. Create `TokenizerME` using the `TokenizerModel` created preceding:

   ```
   TokenizerME tokenizer = new TokenizerME(token_model);
   ```

5. Read the pre-trained sentence detector model `en-sent.bin` provided by Apache OpenNLP and initialize a `SentenceModel`:

   ```
   InputStream sentence_is = new FileInputStream(" \\openNLPdata\\
   models\\en-sent.bin");
   ```

6. Initialize `SentenceModel` using the `InputStream`:

   ```
   SentenceModel sentence_model = new SentenceModel(sentence_is);
   ```

7. Clean up resources:

   ```
   sentence_is.close();
   ```

8. Create `SentenceDetectirME` using the `SentenceModel` created preceding:

   ```
   SentenceDetectorME sdetector = new SentenceDetectorME(sentence_
   model);
   ```

9. Read the pre-trained organization detector model provided by Apache OpenNLP:

   ```
   InputStream org_is = new FileInputStream(" \\openNLPmodels.en\\
   models\\en-ner-organization.bin");
   ```

Initialize `TokenNameFinderModel` using the `InputStream`. This line is loading the name finder model from the disk into the memory. While loading the model, we need to be aware of certain caveats that may cause the model loading to fail:

- The Apache OpenNLP version and the model's version you are trying to load must be compatible

- Make sure you loading the model, that is, `*.bin` files into the appropriate model class

- Make sure the directory or resource where your model resides is accessible

The model format is complaint with Apache OpenNLP format:

```
TokenNameFinderModel org_model = new TokenNameFinderModel(org_is);
```

1. Let's Clean up resources:

    ```
    org_is.close();
    ```

2. Create `NameFinderME` using the `TokenNameFinderModel` created preceding:

    ```
    NameFinderME nameFinder = new NameFinderME(org_model);
    ```

3. We will process our text through the models created and analgise the output. First get the sentences, then loop through each sentence and find the word tokens; pass these token to the name finder API to get the organization names:

    ```
    String sentences[] = sdetector.sentDetect(txt);
    for (String sentence : sentences) {
      String tokens[] = tokenizer.tokenize(sentence);
      Span nameSpans[] = nameFinder.find(tokens);
    ```

4. Print the entity position:

    ```
        for(Span sp : nameSpans){
          System.out.println(sp.toString());
        }
    ```

5. Print organization names:

    ```
    System.out.println("Organization Found: " + Arrays.toString (
    Span.spansToStrings(nameSpans, tokens)));
        }
      }
    }
    ```

The output of the preceding programme is:

```
  Problems   Console ☒   Search   Progress   Debug   History
<terminated> OrganizationFinder [Java Application] C:\Program Files\Java\jdk1.8.0_40\jre\bin\javaw.exe
[0..1) organization
Organization Found: [IBM]
[0..1) organization
Organization Found: [Oracle]
[3..4) organization
Organization Found: [IBM]
[0..1) organization
Organization Found: [Oracle]
```

There are lot of categories in Named entity recognition. We saw organizations in the preceding section; similarly, we can identify the name of a person, name of a place, percentages, money, and so on. Let us look into the R code which does all of it:

1. Load the required libraries:

   ```
   library(rJava)
   library(NLP)
   library(openNLP)
   ```

2. Create a input text which will be used to extract various entities such as person name, place name, percentages, organization name, and money:

   ```
   txt <- "IBM is an MNC with headquarters in New York. Oracle is a
   cloud company in California. James Bond works in IBM. Oracle hired
   John for cloud expertise.
   They give 100% to their profession . Both earn $500000 a year"

   txt_str <- as.String(txt)
   ```

3. Initialize sentence and word tokenizers:

   ```
   sent_token_annotator <- Maxent_Sent_Token_Annotator()

   word_token_annotator <- Maxent_Word_Token_Annotator()
   ```

4. Annotate the text with word and sentence annotators:

   ```
   annotated_str <- annotate(txt_str, list(sent_token_annotator,
   word_token_annotator))
   ```

5. Initialize all the required entity annotators:

```
entity_annotator_org <-Maxent_Entity_Annotator(language = "en",
kind = "organization", probs = FALSE, model = NULL)

entity_annotator_person <-Maxent_Entity_Annotator(language = "en",
kind = "person", probs = FALSE, model = NULL)

entity_annotator_money <-Maxent_Entity_Annotator(language = "en",
kind = "money", probs = FALSE, model = NULL)

entity_annotator_location <-Maxent_Entity_Annotator(language =
"en", kind = "location", probs = FALSE, model = NULL)

entity_annotator_percentage <-Maxent_Entity_Annotator(language =
"en", kind = "percentage", probs = FALSE, model = NULL)
```

6. Create a list of annotators so that applying them to the text will be easy:

```
annotator_list <- list(entity_annotator_person,entity_annotator_
org,entity_annotator_money,entity_annotator_location,entity_
annotator_percentage)
```

7. Run all the annotators through the annotate function:

```
annotated_val <- annotate(txt_str, annotator_list, annotated_str)
```

8. Check the output after annotation:

```
id type       start end features
 1 sentence      1   44 constituents=<<integer,10>>
 2 sentence     46   85 constituents=<<integer,8>>

       .     .     .    .    .    .   .
       .     .     .    .    .    .   .
       .     .     .    .    .    .   .
       .     .     .    .    .    .   .
50 word       207 207
51 word       209 212
52 entity      87  96 kind=person
53 entity     125 128 kind=person
54 entity       1   3 kind=organization
55 entity      46  51 kind=organization
56 entity     107 109 kind=organization
57 entity     112 117 kind=organization
58 entity     199 205 kind=money
59 entity      36  43 kind=location
60 entity      75  84 kind=location
61 entity     162 165 kind=percentage
```

```
Txt_str[annotated_val]
```

```
[1] "IBM is an MNC with headquarters in New York." "Oracle is a cloud company in California."
[3] "James Bond works in IBM."                      "Oracle hired John for cloud expertise."
[5] "They give 100% to their profession ."          "Both earn $500000 a year"
      .      .     .    .      .
      .      .     .    .      .
[51] "year"                                          "James Bond"
[53] "John"                                          "IBM"
[55] "Oracle"                                        "IBM"
[57] "Oracle"                                        "$500000"
[59] "New York"                                      "California"
[61] "100%"
```

9. Let's create a small function that can take the entity name and give us the entities:

```
annotatedVal_txt <- AnnotatedPlainTextDocument(txt_str ,
annotated_val)
getEntityValuesByKind <- function (annotatedTextDoc, kind){
```

10. Get the actual content of the from the doc:

```
text_content <- annotatedTextDoc$content
```

11. Get the annotated data:

```
annotation_data <- annotations(annotatedTextDoc)[[1]]
```

12. Check if the kind parameter is present:

```
if(hasArg(kind)) {
  data_with_features <- sapply(annotation_data$features, `[[`,
"kind")
   text_content[annotation_data[data_with_features == kind]]
  } else {
   text_content[annotation_data[annotation_data$type == "entity"]]
  }
}
```

13. Let's now invoke the function:

```
getEntityValuesByKind(annotatedVal_txt, kind = "person")
```

```
[1] "James Bond" "John"
```

```
getEntityValuesByKind(annotatedVal_txt,  kind ="organization")
```

```
[1] "IBM"    "Oracle" "IBM"    "Oracle"
```

```
getEntityValuesByKind(annotatedVal_txt,   kind ="money")
```

$500000

```
getEntityValuesByKind(annotatedVal_txt,   kind ="location")
```

[1] "New York"   "California"

```
getEntityValuesByKind(annotatedVal_txt,   kind ="percentage")
```

100%

The default models used in the preceding entity recognition code is:

- en-ner-location.bin
- en-ner-money.bin
- en-ner-organization.bin
- en-ner-percentage.bin
- en-ner-person.bin

Training a model with new features

We saw in the preceding example for the input text:

> *"IBM is an MNC with headquarters in New York. Oracle is a cloud company in California. James Bond works in IBM. Oracle hired John for cloud expertise. They give 100% to their profession. Both earn $500,000 a year"*

When we wanted to know the name of the person name and the output was as follows:

```
getEntityValuesByKind(annotatedVal_txt, kind = "person")
```

[1] "James Bond" "John"

What if we change the input text as shown as follows?

> *"Avinash Paul works for a start-up. Anusha was born in London"*

Will the preceding programme identify the names *"Avinash Paul"* and *"Anusha"* ?
Let's experiment with the default model with two text inputs:

- Case 1:

"James Bond works for a start-up. John was born in London"

```
library(rJava)
library(NLP)
library(openNLP)

text <- "James Bond works for a start-up. John was born in London"

text_str <- as.String(text)

sent_token_annotator <- Maxent_Sent_Token_Annotator()

word_token_annotator <- Maxent_Word_Token_Annotator()

annotated_str <- annotate(text_str, list(sent_token_annotator,
word_token_annotator))

entity_annotator_person <-Maxent_Entity_Annotator(language = "en",
kind = "person", probs = FALSE, model = NULL)

annotatedVal <- annotate(text_str, entity_annotator_person,
annotated_str)

annotatedVal
```

- The output of the preceding programme is as follows; we can see it has
  identified two entities as persons:

```
12 word        43  46
13 word        48  49
14 word        51  56
15 entity       1  10 kind=person
16 entity      34  37 kind=person
```

- Case 2:

"Avinash Paul works for a start-up. Anusha was born in London"

Let's look at some short code and its output:

```
library(rJava)
library(NLP)
library(openNLP)

text <- " Avinash Paul works for a start-up. Anusha was born in
London "

text_str <- as.String(text)

sent_token_annotator <- Maxent_Sent_Token_Annotator()

word_token_annotator <- Maxent_Word_Token_Annotator()

annotated_str <- annotate(text_str, list(sent_token_annotator,
word_token_annotator))

entity_annotator_person <-Maxent_Entity_Annotator(language = "en",
kind = "person", probs = FALSE, model = NULL)

annotatedVal <- annotate(text_str, entity_annotator_person,
annotated_str)

annotatedVal
```

- The output of the preceding programme is as follows; the model is not able to identify the names "*Avinash Paul*" and "*Anusha*":

id	type	start	end	features
1	sentence	2	35	constituents=<<integer,7>>
2	sentence	37	62	constituents=<<integer,5>>
3	word	2	8	
4	word	10	13	
5	word	15	19	
6	word	21	23	
7	word	25	25	
8	word	27	34	
9	word	35	35	
10	word	37	42	
11	word	44	46	
12	word	48	51	
13	word	53	54	
14	word	56	61	

The default model `en-ner-person.bin` available in Apache OpenNLP is not trained to identify these names as persons; we have to create another model that is trained to identify these two names as persons. Let's see how to do it by writing a simple Java class. This class trains on data that is in Apache OpenNLP format and has been annotated for the preceding two names.

High-level understanding of the Java code:

- Read the annotated file that is in Apache OpenNLP input format to identify the preceding names as persons
- Invoke the train API exposed by the `NameFinderME` class
- Write the model to the file system:

```
import java.io.BufferedOutputStream;
import java.io.FileInputStream;
import java.io.FileNotFoundException;
import java.io.FileOutputStream;
import java.io.IOException;
import java.nio.charset.Charset;
import java.util.Collections;
import opennlp.tools.namefind.NameFinderME;
import opennlp.tools.namefind.NameSample;
import opennlp.tools.namefind.NameSampleDataStream;
import opennlp.tools.namefind.TokenNameFinderModel;
import opennlp.tools.util.ObjectStream;
import opennlp.tools.util.PlainTextByLineStream;


public class TrainPerson {
```

The main method to invoke the function:

```
public static void main(String[] args) throws IOException {
```

- Path to the annotated text which is the input to the train function.
- Path to the file system where the trained model has to be created.

```
String trainFile = " \\OpenNLP\\test.train";
String modelFile = " \\OpenNLP\\ en-ner-person_custom.bin ";
writePersonModel(trainFile,modelFile);

}
```

The method to train our own model takes two parameters:

- Path to the annotated file
- Path where the model has to be generated:

```
private static void writePersonModel(String trainFile , String
modelFile)
        throws FileNotFoundException, IOException {
```

Set the appropriate character set:

```
Charset charset = Charset.forName("UTF-8");
```

Read the train file, which has the annotated data:

```
FileInputStream fileInputStream = new FileInputStream(trainFile);
ObjectStream<String> lineStream = new PlainTextByLineStream(fileInputS
tream, charset);

ObjectStream<NameSample> sampleStream = new NameSampleDataStream(line
Stream);
```

Initialize `TokenNameFinderModel`:

```
TokenNameFinderModel model;

   try {

model = NameFinderME.train("en", "person", sampleStream,Collections.<S
tring, Object>emptyMap());

}
finally {

    sampleStream.close();

}
```

Write the model to the specified location:

```
BufferedOutputStream modelOut = null;
   try {

   modelOut = new BufferedOutputStream(new
FileOutputStream(modelFile));

   model.serialize(modelOut);
```

```
    } finally {

      if (modelOut != null) {
          modelOut.close();
          }
      }
  }
}
```

The output of the programme is it will generate a model file by the name `en-ner-person_custom.bin` at the specified location. This model can be use in the R code to extract custom entities.

Here is a snapshot of the contents of the train file. I have downloaded a small sample from the web and replaced the names section with my names:

```
<pre>
<START:person> Avinash Paul <END> , 30 years old , 30 years old , will join a start up on Jan. 1  .
<START:person> Anusha <END> is programmer in AhedYou , the data science group .
</pre>
```

Perform the following steps to invoke this `java` class from the R environment:

1. Install the `rJava` package.
2. Initialize the environment.
3. Set the class path with all the relevant jars.
4. Create a JAR file which contains the class methods you want to invoke.
5. Use `rJava` methods to invoke the required methods.
6. Load the required libraries.

The `rJava` package provides the capability of invoking `java` methods, creating objects, accessing fields of java objects through the Java Native Interface in the R environment; in short, it acts as low-level bridge between these two languages.

In order to install this, we need to have JDK installed in our system:

```
install.packages('rJava')
library(rJava)
```

Now let's crank up the **Java Virtual Machine (JVM)**. This function must be called before any `rJava` functions can be used:

```
.jinit()
```

Set the class path. The class path should contain all the `jar` files necessary to execute a given java command; since I have kept my `jar` containing the `TrainPerson` class at `D:/R/testjars`, I am loading that path:

```
.jaddClassPath(dir( "D:/R/testjars", full.names=TRUE ))
```

We can check whether all the necessary jars are in class path by executing the following command:

```
.jclassPath()
```

The output is as shown:

```
[1] "C:\\Users\\avia.ORADEV\\Documents\\R\\win-library\\3.1\\rJava\\java"
[2] "C:\\Users\\avia.ORADEV\\Documents\\R\\win-library\\3.1\\openNLPdata\\java"
[3] "C:\\Users\\avia.ORADEV\\Documents\\R\\win-library\\3.1\\openNLPdata\\java\\jwnl-1.3.3.jar"
[4] "C:\\Users\\avia.ORADEV\\Documents\\R\\win-library\\3.1\\openNLPdata\\java\\opennlp-maxent-3.0.3.jar"
[5] "C:\\Users\\avia.ORADEV\\Documents\\R\\win-library\\3.1\\openNLPdata\\java\\opennlp-tools-1.5.3.jar"
[6] "C:\\Users\\avia.ORADEV\\Documents\\R\\win-library\\3.1\\openNLPdata\\java\\opennlp-uima-1.5.3.jar"
[7] "D:\\R\\chap7\\testjars\\opennlp-maxent-3.0.3.jar"
[8] "D:\\R\\chap7\\testjars\\opennlp-tools-1.5.3.jar"
[9] "D:\\R\\chap7\\testjars\\person_train.jar"
```

Once the jars are loaded, we are good to go; we will create a new instance of the `TrainPerson` class:

```
trainer <- .jnew( "com/train/TrainPerson" )
```

Now we can invoke the required methods present in the `TrainPerson` class by passing all the necessary parameters.

The parameters I am passing to `.jcall` are:

- `Trainer`: The initiated Java object
- `V`: This means the return type is void
- `writePersonModel`: The name of the method that has to be invoked in the `TrainPerson` class

The method takes two parameters: the first parameter is the path to the training data which has the annotated text; the second parameter is the path to the folder where the model file has to be written:

```
.jcall(trainer, "V" , "writePersonModel" , "\\OpenNLP\\test.train" ,
"\\OpenNLP\\ en-ner-person_custom.bin")
```

For making model loading easier, I am creating the new model in the `openNLPmodels.en\\models` directory where all the models are present.

After setting the PATH, relaunch R from the Windows menu; this is necessary and important so that R picks up the PATH changes.

After doing the preceding steps, try:

```
install.packages("rJava")
```

If you use the 64-bit version, make sure that you do not set JAVA_HOME as an environment variable. If this variable is set, rJava will not work. You can check easily within R whether JAVA_HOME is set or not.

To check for JAVA_HOME, use the following command:

```
Sys.getenv("JAVA_HOME")
```

If you need to, you can deactivate JAVA_HOME within your R-session with the following code before loading rJava:

```
if (Sys.getenv("JAVA_HOME")!="")
  Sys.setenv(JAVA_HOME="")
```

To check whether you are running R64, use the following command:

```
.Machine$sizeof.p12/20/2016ointer
[1] 8 this means it a 64 bit version of R
[1] 4 this means it a 32 bit version of R
```

Summary

In this chapter, we learnt about entity extraction and recognition using R implementation of OpenNLP. Also, we learnt to use other functionalities present in Apache OpenNLP but not yet implemented in the OpenNLP package in R.

In the next chapters, we will learn about some real-life applications of the techniques we have learnt so far, on social media data.

Index

reconstruction error 106
R, using for principal component analysis (PCA) 102

discrete random variables
about 4
continuous random variables 5

diverse sources
text, accessing 30

document clustering 135-137

document term matrix
about 19
cosine similarity 21, 22
Damerau-Levenshtein distance 23
edit-distance functions 20
Euclidean distance 20
Gunning frog index 24
Hamming distance 23
inverse document frequency 19
Levenshtein distance 22
words similarity 20

E

Easy Listening Formula (ELF) 67

elements
attributes 91
entities 91
events 91

entity extraction
about 200
machine learning 201, 202
rule-based approach 201

Extensible Markup Language (XML) 36

F

feature extraction
about 91, 92
antonymy 93
concept similarity 94
multiwords 93
negation 93
similarity 92
synonymy 92

feature selection, for text clustering
about 138
frequency-based feature selection 141

mutual information, using 139
statistic Chi Square feature selection 140

file system
about 30
Extensible Markup Language (XML) 36-38
Hyper Text Markup Language (HTML) 35, 36
Hypertext Transfer Protocol (HTTP) 40, 41
JavaScript Object Notation (JSON) 38, 39
Microsoft Word documents 33, 34
PDF documents 30-33

G

generative models 124

H

Hamming distance
about 23
Jaro-Winkler distance 23
text readability, measuring 24

Heaps' laws 13

Hidden Markov Models (HMM), POS tagging
about 77
chunk tags 80
definitions 77, 78
forward algorithm underflow 79
implementing 78
notations 77, 78
OpenNLP chunking 79
Viterbi underflow 79

Hyper Text Markup Language (HTML) 35

Hypertext Transfer Protocol (HTTP) 40

I

independent events
for conditional probability 4

Inverse Document Frequency (IDF) 141

ISOMAP
geodesic distance approximation, calculating 119
using 118

J

JavaScript Object Notation (JSON) 38
Java Virtual Machine (JVM) 227
joint distribution 8

K

kernel functions 174
Kernel Trick 173
kernlab
  implementations 173
  reference 174
k-fold cross-validation 194-196
koRpus package 27

L

language detection 68
language models
  about 15
  hidden Markov models 18
  Markov assumption 17
  N-gram models 16, 17
language package 27
languageR package 14
Latent Dirichlet Allocation (LDA) 125-128
Latent Semantic Analysis (LSA)
  about 131
  example 132, 133
  R package 131
L-BFGS 177
learning curve 191
leave-one-out method 194
lemma 56
lexical diversity
  about 66
  analyse lexical diversity 66
  automated readability index 67
  calculating 67
  readability 67
lexical richness
  about 14
  lexical density 15
  lexical originality 15

lexical sophistication 15
lexical variation 14
linear kernel
  applying 175
linguistics
  quantitative methods 18
lsa package 27

M

Maxent package
  implementing, in R 177, 178
maximum entropy classifiers 175, 176
model evaluation
  about 184
  confusion matrix 184-186
  precision-recall 187
  ROC curve 186
model files
  reference 25
model validation methods
  bootstrapping methods 196
  k-fold cross-validation 194-196
  leave-one-out 194
  stratified sampling 196
multi-word expressions (MWE) 81
multi-word units (MWU) 81
MySQL software
  download link 43

N

named entity recognition
  about 213-222
  model, training with new features 222-231
Natural language processing (NLP) 199
n-fold cross-validation 194

O

occurrences
  counting 10
ODBC Bridge
  download link 46
OpenNLPmodels.language package
  installation link 25

OpenNLP package 25
operations, on document-term matrix
  frequent terms 57
  term association 57
OWLQN 177

P

part-of-speech (POS) 17
pointwise mutual information (PMI) 17
poisson distribution 9, 10
POS tagging
  Hidden Markov Models (HMM) 77
precision-recall 187
precompiled binaries
  download link 30
pre-trained POS models, for OpenNLP
  reference 76
principal component analysis (PCA)
  about 101, 102
  R, using 102, 103
probability
  about 2
  space 2
probability distributions
  R, using 5
probability frequency function 5

Q

quantitative methods, linguistics
  about 18
  document term matrix 19

R

R
  used, for singular vector decomposition
    (SVD) implementation 116, 117
  using, for probability distributions 5
random variables
  about 4
  discrete random variables 4
RcmdrPlugin.temis package 26
Rcurl 40

Receiver Operating Characteristics Curve
    (ROC) 186
reducible error components
  dealing with 192
regular expressions
  used, for processing text 51-55
relation between words, quantifying
  about 84
  contingency tables 84
  detailed analysis, on textual
    collocations 86-91
RKEA package 27
R package, for topic modeling
  about 130
  LDA model, fitting with VEM
    algorithm 130
R packages, text mining
  koRpus 27
  languageR 27
  lsa 27
  maxent 27
  OpenNLP 25
  RcmdrPlugin.temis 26
  RKEA 27
  Rweka 25
  tm 26
R tau package 10
RTextTools 180, 181
R, using for principal component analysis
    (PCA)
  about 102, 103
  Amap package 104, 105
  FactoMineR package 103
  proportion of variance 105
  scree plot function 106
RWeka package 25

S

segmentation 56
sensitivity 186
sentence 56